Politicians, Legislation, and the Economy

ROCHESTER STUDIES IN ECONOMICS
AND POLICY ISSUES

Other titles in the series:

Economics and Social Institutions, edited by Karl Brunner

The Great Depression Revisited, edited by Karl Brunner

Published in cooperation with

The Center for Research in Government
   Policy & Business
Graduate School of Management
University of Rochester
Rochester, New York

POLITICIANS, LEGISLATION, AND THE ECONOMY

An Inquiry into the Interest-Group Theory of Government

ROBERT E. McCORMICK
Graduate School of Management
University of Rochester

ROBERT D. TOLLISON
Center for Study of Public Choice
Virginia Polytechnic Institute
and State University

MARTINUS NIJHOFF PUBLISHING

BOSTON/THE HAGUE/LONDON

DISTRIBUTORS FOR NORTH AMERICA:
Martinus Nijhoff Publishing
Kluwer Boston, Inc.
190 Old Derby Street
Hingham, Massachusetts 02043, U.S.A.

DISTRIBUTORS OUTSIDE NORTH AMERICA:
Kluwer Academic Publishers Group
Distribution Centre
P.O. Box 322
3300 AH Dordrecht, The Netherlands

Library of Congress Cataloging in Publication Data

McCormick, Robert E. 1946–
    Politicians, legislation, and the economy.

    (Rochester studies in economics and policy issues; 3)
    Includes index.
    1. Pressure groups. 2. Income distribution.
I. Tollison, Robert D., joint author. II. Title. III. Series.
JF529.M316   322.4'3   80-25941

ISBN 0-89838-058-8

To Jenny and Anna

CONTENTS

PREFACE

The genesis of this book took place on a hot summer day in College Station, Texas, over four years ago. Sipping our Lone Stars and trying to keep cool, we resolved that we were both tired of the Pigovian fairy tales about government that are so popular among economists. We decided then and there to see if we could come up with an alternative theory of government that would differ radically from the Pigovian approach. In our theory government would not produce anything; it would simply transfer wealth among people. Ours would be the theory that we find in the newspapers every day (private interests) and not the theory that only examines the rhetoric of politicians (the public interest). Ours would be an empirically rich behavioral theory. We would not hide behind *untestable* or *untested* theories. The results of our enterprise follow in this book. We would like to think that the effort has been worthwhile and points the way to a hard-edged, veri-fiable theory of government. This is prejudgment, however; the reader will have his own scorecard.

A number of persons have provided us with helpful insights and suggestions in the course of developing the ideas contained in this book. In this regard we should like to thank our colleagues at Rochester and Blacksburg who provided a friendly and open research environment in which a work such as this could only prosper. Special mention should be made of Armen Alchian, Raymond Battalio, James Buchanan, Mark Crain, John Kagel, Arleen Leibowitz, Cotton Lindsey, John Long, Michael Maloney, Thomas Saving, Clifford Smith, George Stigler, Gordon Tullock, Richard Wagner, and Jerry Zimmerman. We are particularly indebted to Ronald Hansen, who read several drafts of the manuscript and helped us improve the presentation and quality of the argument mightily. We would also like to thank the Center for Research in Government Policy and Business of the Graduate School of Management, University of Rochester, the Center for Study of Public Choice, Virginia Polytechnic Institute, and the National Science Foundation for partial financial support. These various parties are not responsible for the results of our efforts.

1 ANALYZING GOVERNMENT

This is a book about the behavior of politicians in supplying legislation and about how they are remunerated for this activity. The analysis is based on the traditional premise of economic theory that politicians are like other self-interested agents in the economy in that their behavior is influenced mightily by the constraints they face in the pursuit of their self-interest. The questions that the analysis will address are basic and important. How can the activities of legislators be characterized in positive terms? Are they effecting wealth changes in the economy of a zero- or negative-sum kind, or are they passing laws that increase economic welfare? Is it useful to conceive of demand and supply functions for legislation and for groups with a specified interest in legislative outcomes? If legislators can be usefully characterized as brokers of wealth changes mandated through legislation, then what is the supply price, denominated as the sum of the legal and extralegal compensation, required to call forth a given level of their services in this regard? How do the legal and extralegal components of this supply price vary with observable circumstances, such as the occupational composition of legislatures? What roles do competition within a political party and the chief executive play in the brokering of wealth changes? Developing an analysis to answer these and related questions is what this book is about and represents the type of knowledge that the reader may expect to gain from the book.

It almost goes without saying that research along these lines is important and topical. Current and past history are replete with examples of the escapades of legislators, and the behavior of legislators has a dramatic impact on the economy, perhaps more dramatic than the behavior of any other single class of individuals. It is hoped that our analysis, which will be explained more fully below, will offer some useful insights into the behavior of this important group of individuals. We should stress that our urge in writing the book is not reformist but scientific, and the main thing that we hope the reader will carry away from our analysis is a fuller understanding of the role of the legislature in the economy. We will point to certain policy implications if they follow naturally from the analysis (e.g., if you pay politicians more, will malfeasance occur less?), but our book is centered on the idea of understanding how legislators behave and not on designing policies to change legislators' behavior.

Although we are professional economists by training and our analysis proceeds in terms of economic theory and econometrics, the presentation is not at such a formidable level as to deter other social scientists and citizens interested in political behavior from profiting from the book. Indeed, as the reader may surmise for himself, we have gained as much in this inquiry from increasing our knowledge of the inner workings of democratic institutions in the United States, especially at the level of state government, as we have from the formal methods that we have employed to analyze these processes.

A semantic point is appropriate at the outset. Our analysis of politicians is centered upon the concept of wealth transfers mandated through legislation, and we will often speak in such terms. Since there are few laws that do not embody wealth changes (explicitly or implicitly), we view our theory as applicable to a broad class of legislation. Thus, when we say *wealth transfers*, the reader may wish to substitute *issues* or *public policies*. Nothing would be changed in our analysis as a consequence. Yet at the same time we do not claim that we can show that the demand and supply of all legislation are strictly fueled by pecuniary considerations. Some issues stir up emotions and affect utility and are driven by strong nonpecuniary motivations. We recognize the existence and importance of such issues. Our analysis, however, is attuned much more closely to issues that have discernible impacts on individual well-being, and we feel — and it is hoped our argumentation will show — that such issues characterize the great bulk of legislative activity.

TWO APPROACHES TO ANALYZING GOVERNMENT

Economists have worked on two approaches to explaining the role of government in the economy. One approach may be termed the market-failure approach and the other the public-choice, or interest-group, approach. Both routes to analyzing government may be seen as addressing such questions as why government exists and why it undertakes the functions that it performs, and scholars working in these separate frameworks have come to different answers to these basic issues. Our interest here is to distinguish between the two analytical frameworks. After all, the fact that people want government does not indicate why they want it. They could want it to correct a market failure, or to increase their wealth through transfers, or for both types of reasons. It should be clear from the foregoing discussion that we are drawn to the interest-group approach, which we shall apply to the behavior of legislators in this book. Before proceeding to outline the general dimensions of the interest-group model, however, it will be useful to consider the market-failure framework for analyzing government and the various reasons that we feel this approach to be less applicable to the problem that we seek to analyze.

The market-failure approach in modern economics emanates from the work of Pigou.[1] This route to analyzing government stresses the reasons why the market economy fails to function properly in allocating and distributing resources, and suggests that government intervene in the private economy in certain policy-specific ways (taxation) to correct such market failures or distributional shortcomings. In the Pigovian approach the state is a productive entity that produces public goods, internalizes social costs and benefits, regulates decreasing cost industries effectively, redistributes income Pareto optimally, and so forth.

Economists in the public-choice tradition have reacted to the Pigovian approach at a very general level essentially by stressing that it is not a very *believable* theory of government action and, moreover, that it is flawed by the unwarranted assumption that government can be called upon to correct imperfect markets in a perfect and costless manner. That the state is not a perfect instrument for correcting market failures hardly needs demonstration. Whether market or government "failure" is the hallmark of economic history is very much an open question. Indeed, although imperfections in the economy may be lamentable, lamenting is the best that can be done if the consequence of government action is to decrease rather than improve economic welfare.

More specifically, however, the Pigovian approach assumes an all-knowing, benevolent government. It does not answer the question of how the global lack of efficiency or equity in the economy results in any *action* to do something about these problems. The Pigovian approach masks this basic issue without an adequate explanation. Moreover, outside of a few applications of the median voter theorem to policy problems, such as the demand for public goods, the form of government and how this form affects actual practice is not determined in the Pigovian approach.

In essence, therefore, the Pigovians rarely address the costs of program implementation or whether given institutions actually achieve the desired gain in efficiency, and they have left to others construction of the model by which individual demands are linked to collective action. The latter task, of course, is what we hope to accomplish, at least partially, in this work. In doing so, we do not necessarily have to discard the Pigovian framework. Although our analysis will emphasize the proclivity of government agents toward arranging wealth transfers for voters, it is clear that our approach is not necessarily at complete odds with the Pigovian approach. Transfers, after all, can be positive, negative, or zero-sum in character. Government does some things that increase welfare (protection of property rights) and other things that reduce welfare (price controls). Viewed in this light, our analysis is simply a model of the demand and supply of legislation of all varieties, and while we may feel that most of the transfer activities of government fall into the zero- or negative-sum categories, this is, as such, an empirical issue on which we hope to present some persuasive evidence in this book. We are getting ahead of the story a little bit here, however, as it will be useful to discuss some of the general aspects of what we are calling the interest-group approach before proceeding to our analysis.

As we have suggested, the interest-group approach to understanding how governmental agents behave is based on the empirical observation that in many instances there is a sizeable gap between standard economic rationalizations for state intervention in the economy and the actual properties of specific instances of state intervention. Thus while the Pigovian approach rests on the normative presumption that government can increase social welfare by correcting market failures, the interest-group approach is based upon the observed imperfections of governmental "solutions" to private "problems." The interest-group approach thus seeks to develop a scientific understanding of how government agents function under various institutional arrangements in order to explain the divergencies between economic prescription and governmental practice.

The interest-group approach to politics implies that the behavior of political actors within given political institutions can be usefully analyzed by following the guideline that individual economic agents obey the postulates of self-interest generally, whether they are participating in a market or nonmarket setting. Put in so many words, politicians are not different from anyone else. They are economic agents who respond to their institutional environment in predictable ways, and their actions can be analyzed in much the same way as economists analyze the actions of participants in market processes. The important differences between a market and a political setting thus do not consist of the motivations of individual actors. The point is that there is no bifurcation of personality as between our "political" and "private" selves. We do not seek to satisfy the "public interest" when we vote and the "private interest" when we buy groceries. We seek our "self-interests" in both cases. While the story of Dr. Jekyl and Mr. Hyde may make for good cinema, it is a poor basis on which to analyze political behavior.

The important difference between the market and politics consists of the different constraints that face self-interested agents in the two cases. We generally think of the market setting as a proprietary setting where individual agents bear the consequences of their actions directly in terms of changes in their net worth. The political setting, on the other hand, is typically seen as a nonproprietary setting where individual agents do not always bear the full economic consequences of their decisions. Behavior will thus differ in the two settings, not because the goals of behavior are different, but because the constraints on behavior are different.

These are obviously general characterizations and are subject to important exceptions, such as externalities in a private setting. They are, however, useful in pointing to the general theoretical problem involved in distinguishing the market and voting as economic processes. In the literature this problem comes under the heading of the agent-principal problem, and its essence is quite simple. The agent agrees to perform a service for the principal. Because the agent and the principal are both wealth maximizers, it is likely that the agent will not always act in the interest of the principal, particularly if the behavior of the agent is costly to monitor. The agent-principal problem has been analyzed from various perspectives in the literature, with a great deal of interest centered on how contractual and organizational forms have evolved to internalize the malincentives embodied in agent-principal relationships.[2] We need not concern ourselves with the details of this literature here. The point we wish to draw from the agent-principal problem is that political agents will face different constraints on their behavior than private agents because principals in the two cases (e.g., voters and stockholders) face different incentives to control the behavior of the agents. For example, the managers of private firms have increased incentives to control costs in their firms because increased costs come at the expense of firm profitability, and stockholders, by means of such mechanisms as stock options and takeover bids, have the means to discipline managerial behavior toward wealth maximization. Managers of political firms do not face a similar incentive to control costs since they cannot personally recoup any cost saving that they effect for their agencies, and the means available to voters to delimit shirking by political managers are minimal and costly to implement. Thus, our point is simply that political agents will behave differently from private agents because their principals in each case confront them with different sets of constraints.

The point of all this is to stress that public officials are constrained in their behavior by the costs and rewards that they confront. A public agent will no more pursue something called the public interest, as contrasted with pursuing his or her personal interest, than will private agents. Looked at alternatively, is the private high school teacher any less a "public servant" than the public high school teacher? The "public interest" is an outcome of the pursuit of personal interest within a given institutional framework. Private firms in a competitive market adapt their production to the efficient satisfaction of consumer desires not from any self-effacing desire to sacrifice for consumer gain but from recognition that within a competitive institutional framework, this is the way in which they can best enhance their own prosperity. Likewise, the institutional framework of the public economy would seem appropriately to serve as the focal point of analysis. It is the examination of how rational individual conduct is constrained by different institutions that will guide the analysis in this study.

Finally, it should be reemphasized that our analysis will not stress how government *should* act. Granted, formalistic economic theory is replete with arguments based on the concept of a social welfare function in which government employees or legislators somehow overcome human nature and act for the good of all in enacting and administering public policy. We choose, however, to focus on how government acts in practice. Our interest lies in the *positive* questions about how legislators respond to the incentives inherent in their institutional environment and not in *normative* questions concerning what one would like to see government do in terms of one's own values.

THE INTEREST-GROUP THEORY OF GOVERNMENT

This book will apply the interest-group approach to politics to study a specific aspect of political behavior, namely the brokering function provided by politicians in supplying legislation to various groups in the economy. However, prior to turning to the development of this analysis, it will be useful to go over some of the literature on which our analysis will build.

In its broad sense, of course, our analysis will draw upon the many contributions over the years to what has been termed the theory of public choice and the economic approach to politics. However, the specific literature from which this study can be seen as emerging consists of a small body of work by economists on the interest-group theory of government. We thus eschew a broad review of public-choice literature here, especially since good reviews already exist, and concentrate on the relevant papers on the interest-group theory for the purpose of linking this study to previous literature.[3]

In its simple form the interest-group theory of government has been around for quite awhile, primarily in the literature of political science and the early literature of public choice.[4] This theory is often stated in terms of economic regulation because it was designed to explain the pattern of regulatory intervention in the economy. The most elementary (and misleading) form of this theory is normally stated as a "capture theory" of economic regulation. Thus, producers are small enough in number that the potential gains from lobbying for legislative protection from competition will often exceed the costs. Where producers are able to organize to raise price above marginal cost with the aid of the state, their gains come at the expense of consumer-voters generally. Despite the losses in real income that they suffer from monopoly-enhancing legislation, general consumer interests will normally succumb to producer interests because consumers are a large and widely dispersed group that faces relatively high costs of organizing to resist regulations in favor of monopoly.

This simple version of the capture theory is easy to confuse with Marxist theory. It seems to suggest that capital uses the state in a monolithic way in order to transfer income from labor to itself. Yet the confusion with Marxist theory is more apparent than real, and this point became especially clear once economists took hold of the interest-group theory and began to formulate it in a refutable manner. Stigler, who wrote the pioneering paper in this vein, laid out the interest-group theory in terms of the costs and benefits to various groups of using the state to increase their wealth.[5] He showed that it is conceivable under certain configurations of costs and benefits that some large producer groups (e.g., farmers) will find it feasible to seek wealth transfers from the state while some small producer groups (e.g., automobile firms) will organize mainly to resist negative government regulation. Moreover, any group of sellers or buyers, including labor groups, potentially qualifies as an interest group in this more general theory. Stigler thus essentially put the interest-group theory into a testable form and undermined its apparent kinship with Marxism. To emphasize the positive nature of his theory, Stigler presents a variety of evidence that tends to support his outline of the theory of economic regulation.[6]

The most important subsequent contribution to the theory of economic regulation consists of a paper by Peltzman.[7] In this paper Peltzman presents a powerful generalization of Stigler's theory by introducing the role of opposition groups in determining regulatory behavior. He posits a vote-maximizing regulator who must trade off the rents he gives to producers relative to the costs imposed on consumers when he sets a regulated price. Peltzman's contribution thus removes the interest-group theory a step further from the simple capture theory because it demonstrates that regulatory price-setting does not always take place in a way that is profit maximizing to the regulated industry. Peltzman's regulator, however, remains basically a mystery actor in his theory. He presumably maximizes votes in selecting "political" prices, but this is not a very well-defined category of behavior in Peltzman's model.

The last point leads us to where we are going in this book. Our analytical interest in the interest-group theory lies at one stage removed from the theory of economic regulation. That a regulatory agency exists presumes the existence of prior legislation mandating the agency and its operations. Our interest is not in the tug and pull of interests that impinge on regulatory choices as with Stigler and Peltzman, but rather in the forces that drive the political brokers who mandate governmental interference in the economy in the first place.

In this regard there is a small but important literature on the positive economic analysis of legislatures. The basic paper in this literature also is by Stigler.[8] The approach to legislatures taken by Stigler is to consider political processes as analogous to economic processes, that is, subject to the same analysis as any other economic activity. The participants in politics are viewed as utility maximizers operating under different institutional constraints. The outcomes of the "political process" are thus deducible in the context of orthodox economic theory.

Stigler models the sizes of state legislatures as responsive to desires of various group interests. He perceives that representatives are chosen by these interest groups on the basis of the value that the group assigns to the particular policy or law in which they are interested. These values are determined by summing and discounting the net benefits of any particular action over the potentially affected people. Stigler suggests that these valuations have some probability density function, say $f(V_j) = e^{-v}$. Normally, quite a few of these individual evaluations have a small value; that is, they are issues that affect the welfare of individual voters in a trivial way. Some of these issues will, however, have a large value (important issues), and purportedly, the large evaluations are responsible for the selection of representatives.

These valuations are thus perceived as a demand for legislation. Note that this does not necessarily imply that every special-interest group will have its own representatives or that a representative will take care of only one interest group. As Stigler stresses, many groups will have similar interests and hence can use the same representative. Furthermore, the distribution of values is such that in some cases the organizational costs to a group of voters will exceed the discounted present value of representation, and thus these particular groups will not find it efficient to seek representation.

Having taken the view that the political process can be effectively analyzed in a positive framework, Stigler sets out a model of the sizes of state legislatures. He postulates legislative size (for both state senates and houses) as a function of population; rate of change in population; population density; and a dummy variable for New England, which has notoriously large legislatures. His expectations are that larger populations mean more demand for legislators while larger rates of change and higher population densities will imply smaller legislatures. The model turns out to be statistically robust with the exception of the population density variable, and it explains 65 percent of the variation in the size of state houses and 41 percent of the variation in the size of state senates. The same results hold up when the model is applied to lower houses of non-Communist countries.[9] Stigler thus statistically examines the sizes of legislatures as a reflection of the underlying demand for representation, and his results tend to support his theoretical presuppositions.

Stigler concludes his paper with the following observation:

> The foregoing discussion of the sizes of legislatures is long on problems and short on solutions. The problems are commended to economists, not only because of their obvious political importance, but also because these problems in general have counterparts in the organization of economic activity.[10]

What he is suggesting here is that political processes may be quite similar to economic processes and that economists may be able to make significant headway in analyzing politics by applying the same tool kit that they use to analyze market behavior. In fact, Stigler presents a powerful brief for this point of view in an earlier paper.[11] Here, he suggests that the normal tendency of economists to view politics and the market as fundamentally different institutional arrangements is misguided and that the all-or-nothing characterization of political competition is both unappealing and unrealistic. He is more sympathetic to a basic similarity between economic and political competition where, like the market, the output of a political process can be construed as ranging more or less continuously from failure to success. He stresses that there has been a tendency to label (incorrectly) the winning of 51 percent of legislative seats (or anything else) as a victory and 49 percent a defeat. Alternatively, he models the success of a political party as more or less, not all or none.

The really important point of both these papers is that they provide a point of departure from which the interest-group theory of government can be extended. As stressed above, the existing theory of economic regulation is presently developing in terms of how regulatory actors will predictably behave within a given institutional setting. The alternative problem, which is really the essence of the capture theory, is how interest groups form and impact on legislative choice in order to capture rents through state protection from competition. We will analyze this process as a brokerage process, in which the characteristics of the brokerage market (e.g., the size of the legislature) and the pay and occupational background of the brokers (legislators) are important features of the analysis.

We by no means occupy a unique position in attempting to push the literature in this direction. There have been a number of earlier papers along these lines. Perhaps the most important effort to date is the study of the independent judiciary by Landes and Posner.[12] These authors view the independent judiciary as a long-term contracting mechanism in the interest-group theory. Although it is not of direct relevance to the analysis in this study, their argument is nonetheless interesting. They contend that since judicial decisionmakers typically resolve legal disputes by enforcing the desires of the legislature that originally enacted the disputed legislation (an empirical observation), granting the judiciary independence (life tenure) will increase the durability (the present value) of the "contracts" that legislators make with special interests. Moreover, Landes and Posner also examine how the constitutive rules of the legislature can impart durability to legislation and thereby increase the profitability of legislator transactions with special interests. While one may agree or disagree with the Landes-Posner theory of judicial behavior, their examination of the features of the political environment that give durability to legislation represents an important contribution to the development of the interest-group theory.[13]

There are also a number of other contributions to the literature on the economic analysis of legislatures that are a direct outgrowth of

Stigler's recommendation that political institutions be analyzed by analogy to comparable private institutional settings. Like the Landes-Posner theory, these papers are generally not relevant to this inquiry, but for the sake of completeness, they should at least be noted in passing.[14]

PLAN OF THE STUDY

Our study will focus primarily on the role of legislators in matching demanders and suppliers of wealth changes. Our first order of business is therefore to characterize the nature of the "market" for wealth changes and to discuss in a preliminary way how this "market" functions; Chapter 2 is devoted to these tasks. In Chapter 3 we build upon this discussion to specify a theory of the demand and supply of wealth transfers in a representative democracy. Our theory embodies consideration of the formation of interest groups, how these groups will allocate their budgets to maximize the influence they obtain, and how certain characteristics (primarily total size and the ratio of house sizes) of the bicameral vote markets that these groups face impinge upon their influence-maximizing behavior. This model is subjected to several empirical tests using data on state legislative activities in the United States.[15]

With our model of the wealth-transfer process in hand, we proceed in the next several chapters to consider the role of the politician as a broker in this process. In Chapter 4 the nature of the monopoly power of the legislator qua broker is modeled, and this model is tested with respect to the power of the incumbent state legislator to set the level of his legitimate pay. This analysis of political pay is extended in Chapter 5 to develop a theory to explain the outside or extralegal earnings of politicians. This theory is subjected to an empirical test using data on the occupational composition of state legislatures. The nature of competition for positions of party leadership is analyzed in Chapter 6. Chapter 7 is the final substantive chapter of the book, and here we discuss the role of the executive branch (empirically, the governor) in the brokering of wealth changes. A model of gubernatorial compensation is presented and tested. A summary of our major results and some brief concluding observations are offered in Chapter 8.

NOTES

1. See Arthur C. Pigou, *The Economics of Welfare*, 4th ed. (London: Macmillan, 1932).

2. A convenient review of this literature is available in Roger Faith and Robert Tollison, "Contractual Exchange and the Timing of Payment," *Journal of Economic Behavior and Organization*, forthcoming.

3. For a survey of the more general literature on public choice, see Dennis C. Mueller, "Public Choice: A Survey," *Journal of Economic Literature* 14 (June 1976):395–433.

4. For a review of the general literature on this subject, see Richard A. Posner, "Theories of Economic Regulation," *Bell Journal of Economics and Management Science* 5 (Autumn 1974):335–58.

5. See George J. Stigler, "The Theory of Economic Regulation," *Bell Journal of Economics and Management Science* 2 (Spring 1971):3–21.

6. Another important contemporaneous contribution to this theory is a paper by Richard A. Posner, "Taxation by Regulation," *Bell Journal of Economics and Management Science* 2 (Spring 1971):22–50. For other efforts to formulate and test specific applications of the interest-group theory, see Jonathan J. Pincus, *Pressure Groups and Politics in Antebellum Tariffs* (New York: Columbia University Press, 1977); Richard E. Caves, "Economic Models of Political Choice: Canada's Tariff Structure," *Canadian Journal of Economics* 9 (May 1976):278–300; Joel M. Guttman, "Interest Groups and the Demand for Agricultural Research," *Journal of Political Economy* 86 (June 1978):467–84; Elisabeth M. Landes, "The Effect of State Maximum-Hour Laws on the Employment of Women in 1920," *Journal of Political Economy* 88 (June 1980):476–94; and Howard P. Marvel, "Factory Regulation: A Reinterpretation of Early English Experience," *Journal of Law and Economics* 20 (October 1977):379–402.

7. Sam Peltzman, "Toward a More General Theory of Regulation," *Journal of Law and Economics* 2 (August 1976):211–40.

8. See George J. Stigler, "The Sizes of Legislatures," *Journal of Legal Studies* 5 (January 1976):17–34.

9. Even though there is variation in legislative sizes, there is a remarkably small band within which legislative sizes seem to fall. This follows quite easily from the fact that transactions costs increase significantly as size increases in any group arrangement, such as a legislature.

10. Stigler, "The Sizes of Legislatures," p. 31.

11. See George J. Stigler, "Economic Competition and Political Competition," *Public Choice* 13 (Fall 1972):91–106.

12. See William Landes and Richard Posner, "The Independent Judiciary in an Interest-Group Perspective," *Journal of Law and Economics* 18 (December 1975):875–901.

13. For two empirical tests of the Landes-Posner theory, with results favorable to their basic hypotheses, see W. Mark Crain and Robert D. Tollison, "Constitutional Change in an Interest-Group Perspective," *Journal of Legal Studies* 8 (January 1979):165–75; and by the same authors, "The Executive Branch in the Interest-Group Theory of Government," *Journal of Legal Studies* 8 (June 1979):555–67.

14. In particular, see W. Mark Crain and Robert D. Tollison, "Campaign Expenditures and Political Competition," *Journal of Law and Economics* 19 (April 1976):177–88; W. Mark Crain, "On the Structure and Stability of Political Markets," *Journal of Political Economy* 85 (August 1977):829–42; and Robert E. McCormick and Robert D. Tollison, "Legislatures as Unions," *Journal of Political Economy* 86 (February 1978): 63–78.

15. As will become apparent as the analysis of each chapter unfolds, the application and testing of our theory is done with respect to state legislatures in the United States. This approach is followed because data are readily available on these legislatures and on other economic characteristics of states. State governments thus provide a natural cross-sectional laboratory for testing our propositions about wealth changes and political brokers. The principles that we derive are, of course, general principles, capable of being applied to any democratic setting.

2 QUESTIONS TO BE ANSWERED

The interest-group theory of government is based upon the premise that a major portion of governmental activity is devoted to the transfer of resources among citizens. Some citizens are net winners in this process and some are net losers. Moreover, the wealth-transfer process is not a simple process in which well-organized and wealthy producers increase their wealth through legislation at the expense of widely dispersed and poorly organized consumers. The more generally correct characterization of the wealth-transfer process does not pit consumers against producers but allows each economic unit to seek transfers from the other units in the economy-polity. Our primary interest in this process will be to analyze the role of the political representative in *brokering* transfers among the various groups in a society.

In one sense the political middleman is analogous to his counterpart in a private setting. Politicians get paid for pairing suppliers and demanders of wealth transfers, that is, for reducing information costs in the market for wealth transfers. However, unlike many of their private sector counterparts (e.g., agricultural middlemen), the process of entry

into the occupation of political representation is not "free." Indeed,
entry into the market for political representation is governed by relatively strict constitutional rules; for example, successful entry requires
approval by a simple majority or plurality of voters.[1]

Entry barriers in politics must be interpreted cautiously, however.
There are a large number of people who compete to become political
middlemen, and as we shall see, there are distinct advantages from
this competition.[2] The interesting questions from our point of view
concern how elements of political competition are manifested in political behavior and, moreover, what are the positive economic explanations of competitive and noncompetitive outcomes in the market for
political brokers of wealth transfers.

WEALTH TRANSFERS AND ORGANIZATION COSTS

A discussion of wealth transfers by a representative government must
be predicated on the existence of certain information and transaction
costs. Without the existence of such costs wealth would never be
willingly given up by an individual unless such a transfer were Pareto-
superior in nature — that is, in a costless world all equilibrium states
will be Pareto-optimal, and only welfare-enhancing transfers would be
enacted by political representatives. When positive (and differential)
information and transaction costs exist, some groups will be able to
organize and acquire information more cheaply than others, and these
differences among groups will give rise to a demand and supply of
wealth redistributions (see the Appendix to this chapter for further
discussion of this point). Consider some of the implications of these
costs for our analysis.

No Pareto-inferior policies will be adopted where a unanimity rule
governs political decisions and voting is costless. As we move away
from this idealized setting toward a world of costly voting, transfer-
seeking activities will become more prevalent. Some voters may even
shirk and allow some of their wealth to be taken away under a unanimity rule if the costs of voting exceed the benefits. Majority rule will
raise the amount of transfer-seeking because it lowers the costs of
influencing collective decisions. As we stressed above, however, the
key to understanding transfer seeking lies in the costly voting side of
the problem — namely, What is the nature of the information and

organization costs facing voters to effect a political decision in a majority-rule regime?

The individual faces basically two types of information costs in transfer seeking: He must discover the effects of an issue on his personal wealth, and he must identify other individuals who will join him on the issue. Several possibilities are relevant in this regard: (1) The winners and losers on an issue are well identified and know who each other are; (2) the winners and losers are not easily identified, either to themselves or to each other; (3) obviously, winners can be easily identified while losers cannot, and conversely. The positive implication that follows from this taxonomy of information costs is the well-known result that more wealth transfers are expected in a category such as (3). Political brokers will have incentives to search for this type of issue, which in general represents the traditional model of well-organized groups gaining transfers at the expense of the general polity. In this case the winners are easily identified, and the losers poorly identified. Moreover, the losers may lose on an issue only in an opportunity cost sense (for example, the value of deregulation), they may find the benefits of deregulation hard to predict, and they may find it not worthwhile on an individual basis to invest in procuring deregulation.

A second general point about organization costs is that these costs are like start-up costs. Once they are borne, they do not affect marginal costs (though if the "firm" is to survive, they must be borne over time). Groups that have already borne these start-up costs, for reasons unrelated to lobbying, will have a comparative advantage in seeking transfers and will therefore be more successful in procuring transfers as a result. This is simply a point about jointness in production. Some groups will be able to produce political lobbying as a by-product of performing some other function, thereby avoiding start-up costs for lobbying. There are many examples of such groups in the economy, among which are labor unions, trade associations, corporations, and the like.[3]

In addition to organization and information costs there is another category of costs related to our analysis that are due to the potential for individuals to "free ride" on the costly lobbying efforts of others. Within each of the $(2^n - 1)$ coalitions in our theory (see note 5), there is a cost associated with collective action, and any one participant may receive some of the benefits of collective action without bearing his share of the costs. The groups that emerge to lobby in our theory will thus find it useful to devise institutions that mitigate free riding by members. For example, organized labor relies upon union halls, labor bosses, and national federations to bring forth a supply of votes from members. Labor union members will vote because they know that other members will vote and their votes will therefore count. In effect, each member knows that his probability of voting will affect other members' probabilities of voting, and this fact helps to overcome the free-riding problem in lobbying. A more homely example of the same point is the use of collection plates in churches. Contributions are made more visible to reduce free-riding costs.[4]

THE "MARKET" FOR WEALTH TRANSFERS

Suppose that we order all possible combinations of individuals, from each individual to all possible individuals in the economy-polity, and then rank these combinations of individuals from a highest to a lowest value in terms of their demand for wealth transfers.[5] That is, we ask each group what they would bid for a dollar of transfers, net of their costs of organizing, becoming informed, and overcoming free-rider problems to receive these transfers.[6] As in the usual case, this demand curve is negatively sloped. Such a demand curve (D) is drawn in Figure 2–1. Note that although it is not important in general, this demand curve can be negative for some individuals or groups that have sufficiently high organization costs.

The derivation of D is straightforward. Each of our ($2^n - 1$) coalitions would pay one dollar for one dollar of transfers *before* we net out their costs of organizing, becoming informed, and overcoming free riders. The horizontal line in Figure 2–1 at the level of $1 represents these identical valuations by each of the groups in the economy-polity. From the $1 line, we *subtract* each group's costs of engaging in collective action to derive its *net* demand price for transfers, which is given by D in Figure 2–1. For example, the ($n + k$)th coalition has organization costs equal to the vertical distance, AB, and a demand price of $P_{(n+k)}$.

Within this setting consider the role of political representatives in terms of an analogy. Suppose that the representatives have a preexisting, community-financed police force that can compel all the groups in the economy-polity to enter a brokerage house and engage in trades.

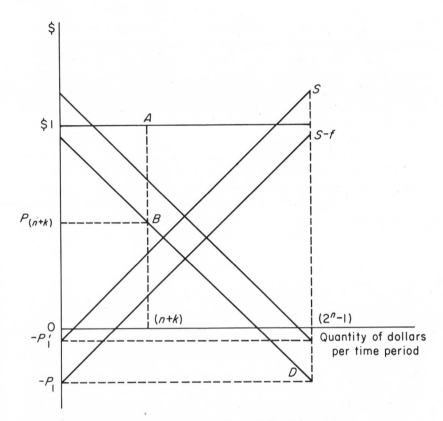

Figure 2–1. Demand and Supply of Wealth Transfers

This assumption obviously parallels the coercive nature of politics (you cannot refuse to pay taxes). The police force, however, does not compel any particular pattern of trades. Further, assume that the political broker imposes a fee equal to the marginal cost of the real resources used in transacting in the brokerage house — for example, the building, the heating, lighting, and so forth — and assume that this fee is constant over all ranges of transactions.

From the demand curve in Figure 2–1 and from the brokerage fee, f, we can derive a supply curve of wealth transfers. The supply curve begins at point $(2^n - 1)$ in Figure 2–1, with a supply price equal to the nth group's demand price $(-P_1)$ plus the brokerage or trading fee, f. Put another way, the cheapest unit available for transfer is available at $-P_1'$ ($-P_1' = -P_1 + F$). The supply curve of wealth transfers is read from right to left and is nothing more than an inverse demand curve for wealth transfers plus the political brokerage fee. In fact, we can make Figure 2–1 look like a conventional demand and supply diagram by mapping the mirror image of the supply of transfers (S). This is done in Figure 2–2, where $S - f$ is the inverse demand curve *without* the brokerage fee included.

There are quite obviously "gains from trade" (keep in mind that trade is coerced) in wealth transfers in this model as depicted in Figure 2–2. Some groups have high demand prices for transfers relative to other groups. Given a fixed fee of transacting in this model, there is a single demand price, P^*, that equates quantity demanded with quantity supplied, $Q_D = Q_S = Q^*$. Groups with demand prices less than

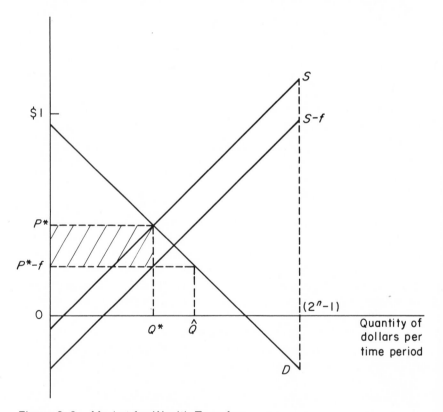

Figure 2–2. Market for Wealth Transfers

$P^* - f$ will be suppliers of wealth transfers at a rate of a dollar per group [i.e., $(2^n - 1) - \hat{Q} = 0Q^*$]. Being compelled by the brokers' police force to organize or transfer, they find it cheaper to transfer their dollars. Groups with marginal evaluations greater than P^* will receive a transfer of one dollar per group, that is, $0Q^* = (2^n - 1) - \hat{Q}$. Groups with marginal evaluations below P^* but greater than $P^* - f$, that is, those who lie between Q^* and $\hat{Q}$, will be undisturbed by the wealth-transfer process due to the real resource costs of transacting. Real resources equal to $f \cdot (0Q^*)$, or the shaded area in Figure 2–2, are consumed in reaching a "market-clearing" level of wealth transfers. Note that this only includes the real resources consumed in operating the brokerage house and not the costs of winners and losers engaging in transfer activities.

The nature of "price" in this model needs to be clarified. The suppliers of wealth transfers do not receive the demand price, P^*, in this case. This compensation goes to the political broker and the successful transfer seekers, since the broker is by assumption in charge of the scarce resource (police power) necessary to compel wealth transfers, and he in turn is supported, in office, by the net demanders. This payment need not be in cash. To the broker, votes may be a convenient form of barter. The suppliers of transfers receive a return that must be denominated in opportunity cost terms. By allowing their wealth to be taken away, they avoid the time and trouble of organizing to resist the power of the brokers to take away their dollars and give them to other groups. This return is valued proximately at $P^* - f$. Given that a constitution, a government, a power to tax exist, these suppliers are paid in resources they do not have to spend. By paying their taxes or monopoly prices due to government regulation, they receive a "payment" from the state in excess of the value of those taxes — namely, they do not have to bear organization and free-riding costs that, by construction, are greater than their tax burden or wealth loss. Finally, the marginal demander must pay the broker P^* and is therefore indifferent between receiving a transfer and paying the broker. Because of the assumption of a single price for brokering services, all other (net) demanders of transfers receive a transfer worth more to them than they pay for it. What this means is that the price, P^*, is just a demarcation of the transfer seekers into "winners" and "losers."

It should be clear that we model the political sector as an ongoing process of wealth-transfer *flows*. Unless there is some exogenous change in organization costs, our market-clearing "price" will persist indefinitely. For example, suppose in Figure 2–1 that the quantity of transfers exceeded the market-clearing level of Q^*. Groups that are losing wealth will pay more to prevent these losses than the transfers are worth to them, and groups that are receiving transfers will receive less than the costs of supplying the transfers to them. The political market is out of equilibrium because politicians have transferred too much wealth. Politicians will thus be voted out of office, platforms will change, and so forth until equilibrium is restored where the price of transfers equates the quantity demanded with the quantity supplied.

WHAT THIS ANALYSIS IS NOT ABOUT

Perhaps most importantly, our analysis is not about public goods. Government does not produce anything in our model; it is simply a wealth-transfer process. The model could, however, be adapted easily to the idea of government producing public goods. For example, our demand for wealth transfers could be seen as a demand for political services. In this respect the demand for political services would have all the same characteristics as the demand for wealth transfers. It is downward sloping to the right, and it lies inside the vertical sum of individual marginal evaluations due to such factors as free-riding costs. This is, of course, the standard approach to public-goods analysis in the literature, and we see no good reason to repeat this familiar analysis. We choose instead to go forward with our model of government as a wealth-transfer process and see how far it can carry us in the study of how political institutions function. Perhaps our approach will lead to a richer and more readily verifiable theory of government than the public-goods approach. At least we would ask readers to grant us the license to pursue our approach and to ascertain its scientific value.

Moreover, it should be clear that we abstract (as do all model builders) from various practical aspects of politics in our highly stylized model of a Marshallian representative bill. There are no issues, no bills, no face-to-face confrontations between protagonists, no Democrats, and no Republicans in our theory. Our market for wealth transfers is like the grain market. A certain amount of "grain" is brought to the market each day, demanded, and consumed. In our approach issues are just manifestations of wealth transfers and can take any form, ranging from cash transfers to highways, schools, and the like. Winners and losers in the transfer process can only be identified *ex post,* after the model (P^*) has decided who they are. We could go on in this vein, but the point is simply to caution the reader about the types of problems that we do not address in our approach. This done, we can now turn to outlining our primary concerns in the analysis of the wealth-transfer process.

WHAT THIS ANALYSIS IS ABOUT

Our primary purpose in modeling wealth transfers in this chapter is to focus attention on the role of the political representative as analogous to a broker in the wealth-transfer process. Moreover, our interest in politicians as brokers does not center around the fact that the act of arranging political trades involves the use of real resources, for example, the provision of a building where trade can take place. Rather, our interest in political brokering resides in the nature of the "price" paid to politicians for their brokering services.

Consider the following example of the type of question we propose to address. Imagine that certain individuals have a comparative advantage at being compensated as political brokers; in other words, demanders of wealth transfers can pay these people more easily than they can pay other individuals for arranging political trades. In terms of the above model suppose that some "brokerage houses" are also grocery stores. Demanders of wealth transfers visit grocery stores daily, and hence an extra trip is not required in order to compensate the political broker for wealth transfers received. In this setting our expectation would be that the individuals who have a comparative advantage at selling groceries would simultaneously have a comparative advantage at political brokering, other things the same. One type of question we are interested in, therefore, concerns the prevalence of certain occupational backgrounds (e.g., lawyers and farmers) among legislators as political brokers.

Moreover, we do not mean to suggest that there is an absence of competition in the market for political brokers. Competition is a powerful force in this market and is manifested in a variety of ways. Political parties and the competition within and among them are perhaps the best known forms of political competition. Generally, however, when economists talk about competition among private firms, certain efficiency implications follow. For example, competition allocates resources to their most highly valued uses and allocates production in a least-cost manner. Such implications do not necessarily carry over to the political market where majority rule and attenuated property rights prevail.

In a representative democracy voters-taxpayers can be considered as analogous to owners (principals) and politicians as analogous to managers (agents). Elections are a means to choose a set of political managers to operate the governmental enterprise until the next election. Two points are crucial about elections. First, the right to run the government is *not* auctioned off to the highest bidder. It is granted in a voting process, the characteristics of which will vary with the particular representative democracy in question. As is well known, not only will the size of bids from potential political agents to voters be important but their distribution among voters will be crucial in determining the outcome of majority voting processes. A major difference, then, between voting and the market is that the highest bidder will not necessarily win the contract to manage the "firm." Second, voters-taxpayers as owners of the contract bundle that defines the potential output of government have no way to liquidate their ownership rights. That is, unlike the owners of private firms, voters cannot sell the right to use their contract bundles to politicians in an exchange for a payment before productive activity begins. Contract owners in politics do not get paid until after the fact of production, and then they typically receive their payment in kind rather than in cash.

The point is that society has selected a method of choosing political agents (one man–one vote) that does not lead to efficient outcomes in the same sense that such outcomes are produced in private competitive markets. While political competition may generate efficiency in the broad and largely tautological sense of agents behaving efficiently in the face of given constraints, there is no necessary connection between political competition and what economists normally refer to as economic efficiency. Our concern, however, is not with the normative quality of the outcomes produced by political competition. We accept that competition is a powerful force in politics, and our primary concern is to seek the deductive implications of these competitive forces and to test them empirically.

By analyzing the price paid for political brokering and the impact that differing institutional arrangements (e.g., term lengths) have on this price, we will be able to shed some light on a variety of interesting questions. Can a consistent and testable model of government as a wealth-transfer process be formulated? Who gets to be a broker in this process? Are there inframarginal rents associated with the brokerage function? Why do we observe differing rules of the game (constitutions) across political jurisdictions, and can anything be said about the impact of such differences on the extent of wealth-transfer activities? These are but a few of the questions that we propose to examine based upon the model of wealth transfers and political middlemen presented in this chapter.

SUMMARY

The discussion in this chapter concentrated on defining the nature of the demand and supply of wealth transfers and on the role of the legislature in effecting such redistributions. This discussion was presented in the form of a preliminary analysis of the wealth-transfer process and was employed primarily to define the type of questions about the role of legislators as brokers in this process that will be addressed in the remainder of this book.

APPENDIX: HETEROGENEITY BEGETS WEALTH REDISTRIBUTION

As a limiting example of the model in this chapter, consider the case where every group in the polity has equal organization costs. Let this net of costs evaluation be k. Under these conditions the demand curve for transfers will be flat at k and will extend from 1 to $(2^n - 1)$. The supply curve will be perfectly elastic at $k + f$, and there is no price that equates quantity supplied with quantity demanded. Hence, if the community is composed of n clones, there will be *no* transfers forthcoming under these conditions. The moral is obviously that differential organization costs among individuals and groups are the basis for wealth redistribution. Heterogeneity begets redistribution.

Consider Figure 2–3, which is similar to Figure 2–1 in that demand is read left to right and supply right to left. When the demand curve is D_0 (perfectly elastic), there will be no transfers. In fact, there will be no transfers unless the evaluation (net of organization costs) of the

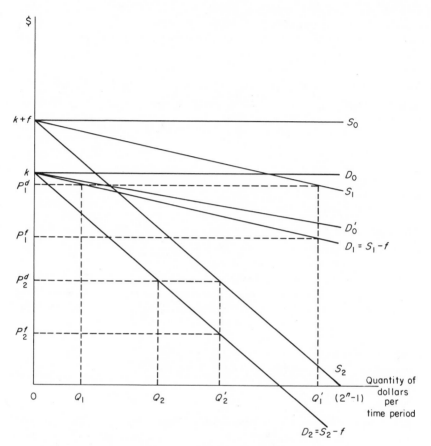

Figure 2–3. Elasticity of the Demand for Transfers

$(2^n - 1)$ group is less than the evaluation of the first group less the transaction fee, f. So unless the demand curve is more inelastic than D'_0, there will be no transfers.

Holding organizational costs constant, we can imagine that increasing the degree of heterogeneity (in whatever dimension) amounts to rotating the demand curve through some point (not necessarily the vertical intercept). As this is done, we see that transfer activity increases from zero to $Q_1 = [(2^n - 1) - Q'_1]$ when demand is D_1, and to $Q_2 = [(2^n - 1) - Q'_2]$ when demand is D_2.

Finally along these lines, we can assume that the degree of homogeneity is constant in this formulation and increase organization costs.[7] This procedure again amounts to a clockwise rotation of the demand curve. As before, we see that the quantity of transactions increases and the price falls (!). In fact, the price could even fall to zero if organization costs were sufficiently high.

NOTES

1. See Gordon Tullock, "Entry Barriers in Politics," *American Economic Review* 55 (May 1967):458–66.
2. Recall, however, that as George J. Stigler ("The Sizes of Legislatures," *Journal of Legal Studies* 5 [January 1976]:17–34) shows, the sizes of legislatures across states are quite similar and are basically insensitive to changes in the level of economic activity. Political competition thus does *not* take the form of expansions in the sizes of legislatures but rather of "competition for the field." On the latter, see Tullock, "Entry Barriers in Politics."
3. Some individuals will find that their private activities intersect with politics in a complex way involving more than one interest group; other individuals will find their lobbying interests effectively represented by a single interest group. Clearly, organization costs are higher where one's political interests span a larger number of interest groups (the individual, for example, must keep track of more issues), and we would expect such diffuse interests to be less successful in organizing to gain transfers than the more concentrated efforts of a group of individuals dedicated to pursuing a single type of transfer.
4. For the general analysis underlying this discussion, see George J. Stigler, "Free Riders and Collective Action: An Appendix to Theories of Economic Regulation," *Bell Journal of Economics and Management Science* 5 (Autumn 1974):359–65.
5. In a group of n individuals there are ($2^n - 1$) possible coalitions.
6. Initially, we shall restrict each group to demanding and supplying only one unit of transfer, that is, one dollar. The model is perfectly general in this respect. It can be seen as a model of the demand for transfers over all issues or on a single issue. We also ignore the fact that organization costs may vary with respect to the type of transfer sought.
7. For simplicity, assume that the group with the highest evaluation for transfers experiences no increase in organization costs so that we can rotate the demand curve through the vertical axis.

3 THE DEMAND AND SUPPLY
OF WEALTH TRANSFERS

Based on the concepts laid out in the first two chapters, we see that wealth transfers to successful interest groups are inexorably linked to shirking by voters. In a world of costless voting and Wicksellian unanimity there would clearly be no Pareto-inferior moves; all transfers would enhance individually perceived welfare. Costly voting encourages transfer-seeking activity because it makes shirking efficient for some voters; indeed, some voters may even shirk under a unanimity rule if the costs of voting and becoming informed exceed the benefits of voting. Individuals will thus let their wealth be taken away from them so long as the costs of changing political outcomes are less than the amount of wealth taken away. If collective decisions are easily influenced, there will be a small amount of wealth transfers

A shorter version of this chapter was originally published in Robert E. McCormick and Robert D. Tollison, "Wealth Transfers in a Representative Democracy," in *Toward a Theory of the Rent-Seeking Society,* James M. Buchanan, Robert D. Tollison, and Gordon Tullock, eds. (College Station: Texas A&M University Press, 1980), pp. 293–313.

supplied. As the costs of monitoring and sanctioning collective decisions rise, a larger quantity of wealth transfers will be supplied.

Where there are costs associated with obtaining wealth transfers, not all individuals or groups will find it worthwhile to seek them. Individuals or groups who do find such activity profitable are customarily called lobbyists or interest groups. The purpose of this chapter is to develop more fully the theory of lobbying behavior by interest groups in the pursuit of wealth transfers. This theory will be expressed in terms of a maximization process in which the lobbyist seeks to maximize the returns to his interest group (net of total lobbying expenses) from legislation.[1] A model is presented in the next section where we derive the conditions that indicate how the lobbyist will allocate his lobbying budget in a bicameral vote market to maximize his interest group's returns from legislation. Moreover, the properties of this model when the size of the legislature and the relative sizes of the two houses of the legislature change are also developed. A number of testable implications come from this analysis. Perhaps the primary ones are that the lobbyist will fare better in procuring returns from legislation for his interest group where the size of the legislature is smaller and where the sizes of the senate and house are more equal. These implications of the analysis, along with several others, are subjected to several empirical tests in the second section below. Some summary remarks conclude the chapter.

MAXIMIZING THE RETURNS FROM LEGISLATION IN A BICAMERAL VOTE MARKET

Initially, we follow Stigler's lead in stressing that legislative influence is analogous to market influence and that it is not appropriate to think in strict majoritarian terms when analyzing the concept of political influence.[2] In this part of the analysis the activity of the lobbyist is analyzed in terms of how he derives and allocates his budget in the buying of legislative influence to maximize the returns to his interest group from legislation. There is no presumption that the lobbyist has to buy a majority of legislators in order to reap returns from legislation. Later in the section the analysis is recast into terms of purchasing a simple majority of legislators in both houses. In either case the presumption of an economic approach to the market for special-interest legislation is that increasing levels of expenditures by an interest group will increase the influence or votes that the group receives on an issue. The naive view that influence in one chamber is useless without influence in the other is thus rejected.

A second introductory point is that although it could be argued that demand and supply factors generate a single market-clearing price of legislation, it should be clear that each piece of legislation will not evoke uniform support or opposition. Small groups or groups that face low costs of controlling free-riding behavior among their members can offer politicians greater support (e.g., campaign contributions and votes) in return for the support of politicians on legislation. The amount of influence purchased per dollar will vary among interest groups as their ability to support politicians varies; in other words, every piece of legislation will have a different demand and supply function so that practically speaking, each legislative transaction will carry a separate price. This argument will be developed more formally later in this section when considerations of the size of the interest group are introduced.

Theory

The interest group must decide how much to spend on buying legislative influence, and its agent must decide how to allocate this budget across the two houses of the legislature so as to maximize the organization's returns from legislative influence. Whether the group can "afford" the price necessary to win returns through legislation will again be a function of its comparative advantage in collecting votes and contributions for politicians. The organization knows that the votes (V) it will receive in each house are a function of its expenditures in each house (E^h and E^s) and the size of each house (h and s) — that is, $V^h = V^h(E^h, h)$ and $V^s = V^s(E^s, s)$. The economic problem faced by the interest group is therefore to maximize the net returns (Y_n) from legislative influence — that is, $Y_n = Y - E$, where E is the size of the group's lobbying budget.

$$Y_n = Y - E, \qquad (3\text{-}1)$$

$$E = E^h + E^s, \qquad (3\text{-}2)$$

$$Y = Y(V^h, V^s, L, W, P), \qquad (3\text{-}3)$$

where Y_1, Y_2, Y_4, $Y_5 > 0$, and $Y_3 < 0$.

$$V^h = V^h(E^h, h), \qquad (3\text{--}4)$$

$$V^s = V^s(E^s, s). \qquad (3\text{--}5)$$

where V_1^h, V_2^h, V_1^s, $V_2^s > 0$; V_{11}^h, V_{22}^h, V_{11}^s, $V_{22}^s < 0$; and V_{12}^h, $V_{12}^s > 0$.

Equation (3–3) maps the levels of house and senate influence, V^h and V^s, into income. Increasing levels of influence enhance the returns from lobbying (Y_1, $Y_2 > 0$). Rather than votes, influence is employed as a more general measure of what interest groups seek. The degree of correspondence between influence and votes will be a function of the homogeneity of legislators. If legislators are identical and come from identical districts, influence and votes will be equivalent. However, if legislators are different (e.g., they have different term lengths), their ability to manipulate political processes will vary and the correspondence between influence and votes will diverge. In this case, which is the one most frequently observed, the purchase of influence by an interest group is the more general case and will be formalized first. The purchase of votes is a special case of the purchase of influence; it will be analyzed later in this section.

The wealth (W) of a community influences lobbying in two ways. As wealth increases, the costs to individual voters of monitoring the political process increase (a substitution effect), and the income obtained by a lobbying group should thus rise in wealthier jurisdictions. However, if monitoring the political process is an income-elastic consumption good, an argument often made, there is an income effect of increasing community wealth on monitoring that cuts in the opposite direction from the substitution effect. In our analysis we will claim that the substitution effect dominates ($Y_4 > 0$).

As population (P) increases, the probability of any one voter's influencing collective decisions decreases. Moreover, for a given transfer (W^0) the per capita share of the costs falls as P increases. For both these reasons more transfers will be forthcoming from larger populations ($Y_5 > 0$).

Legislative size (L), which is $h + s$, has an important effect on the interest group's returns from legislation; this effect is examined in detail below.

Equations (3–4) and (3–5) are the vote production functions in the two houses. These vary as the institutional character (e.g., term lengths) of the two houses varies. We assume that there are diminishing returns of influence, wealth, and population on income in each house and across both houses taken together. The presumption of diminishing returns in equations (3–3), (3–4), and (3–5) is based upon two arguments.

The first argument derives from our earlier discussion about each piece of legislation carrying a separate price. As various legislators arrive from different constituencies, their relative prices to interest groups, based on potential campaign support by the various groups, will result in an ordering of supply prices among legislators; in other words, the political transfer process must pay careful attention to the opposition (or "losers") so that at the margin the political gain to the politician from the last dollar transferred just equals the loss.[3] Since an interest group will first purchase the legislative influence that carries the lowest supply price, there are diminishing returns of expenditures to votes, as given in equations (3–4) and (3–5). Second and similarly, an interest group will first convert its influence into the projects that have the greatest impact on its income. We assume that the various legislation that an interest group seeks will have descending impacts on its income and that there are therefore diminishing returns of influence to income. It will turn out that diminishing returns in either case is a necessary condition for a determinate solution to the optimal level of spending (E) by an interest group.

For several reasons legislative size plays an important role in the lobbying process. First, increasing legislative size increases the number of vote suppliers and reduces the costs of influence or votes. Since in this theory politicians are brokers between winners and losers in the wealth-transfer process, the degree of competition in the legislative process will affect their brokerage fee. As some analysts have argued, the presence of a few firms does not necessarily imply a noncompetitive outcome.[4] What it does suggest, however, is a relatively low cost of colluding. The latter point is especially important in the case of a legislature where entry is not costless and the size of the legislature is fixed. For such reasons increases in house size will reduce the price of influence because of reduced monopoly power among suppliers, but this effect should diminish quite rapidly ($V_2^h, V_2^s > 0$); in other words, for a fixed level of lobbying expenditures in either chamber, a larger house size will increase the level of absolute influence obtained and perhaps, but not necessarily, the proportion of influence obtained, in both cases at a diminishing rate. Second, there is a perhaps more important effect of legislative size due to the fact that larger legislatures mean smaller relative influence for any individual legislator. This might be termed the small-fish-in-the-big-pond effect. Larger legislatures are thus characterized by relatively weak individual legislators, weak in the sense that the influence of any one of them is likely to have a small impact on the income of a lobbying group. The third reason (perhaps an insignificant one) is that a larger legislature reduces the number of voters per legislator, and this might lead to improved policing by voters. Another way of saying the same thing is to argue that larger legislatures will more closely represent the entire citizenry, and hence there will be a smaller level of wealth transfers supplied under these circumstances. (Consider the limiting case where all voters are in the legislature.) It is less expensive for losers in the wealth-transfer process to affect political outcomes when legislative size is large; thus, when legislative size increases, an interest group will find that its fixed stock of votes or influence yields fewer transfers.

We capture these effects in equation (3–3) by signing $Y_3 < 0$; that is, as legislative size increases, any particular absolute amount of influence obtained, V^h and V^s, will be less valuable because in a relative sense the influence obtained has actually declined.[5]

If we insert equations (3–2) through (3–5) into equation (3–1), we find that the first-order conditions necessary to maximize the group's net income with choice variables E^h and E^s are

$$Y_1[V^h(E^h, h), V^s(E^s, s), L, W, P] \, V_1^h(E^h, h) = 1, \qquad (3\text{–}6)$$

and

$$Y_2[V^h(E^h, h), V^s(E^s, s), L, W, P] \, V_1^s(E^s, s) = 1. \qquad (3\text{–}7)$$

These two conditions taken together imply that

$$\frac{V_1^h(\cdot)}{V_1^s(\cdot)} = \frac{Y_2(\cdot)}{Y_1(\cdot)}, \qquad (3\text{–}8)$$

or that the lobbying group will spend to influence votes until the ratio of the marginal impact of its expenditures on votes in the two houses equals the ratio of the marginal impact of relative votes in the two houses on its income.[6]

A Graphical Illustration

We can illustrate this analysis graphically. The upper panel of Figure 3–1 shows the "production functions" of votes in a bicameral legislature. The number of votes that the expenditures of a lobbyist will

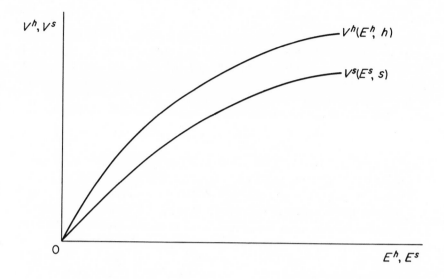

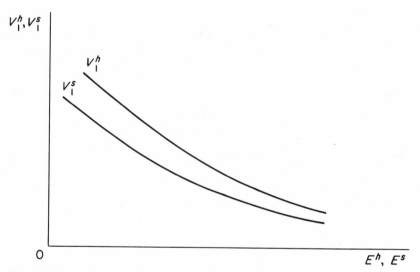

Figure 3–1. Influence or Production Functions

win is a function of these expenditures and the size of each chamber. Without loss of generality we assume that $h > s$. There are consequently a larger number of vote suppliers in the lower house, and each supplier has less monopoly power. We therefore assume that equal expenditures by the lobbyist will produce a larger vote in the house relative to the senate — that is, $V^h(E^0, h) > V^s(E^0, s)$, if $h > s$ for all E. The lower panel of Figure 3–1 shows the marginal impact of lobbying expenditures in each house, and we again assume that $V_1^s(E^0, s) < V_1^h(E^0, h)$, if $s < h$ for all E.

In Figure 3–2 we show the effect of lobbying expenditures on gross income through votes. Panel I shows the relationship between expenditures and votes (as in Figure 3–1), and panel II maps these votes into income. Following the above discussion, we assume that votes in the smaller house, s, have a greater impact at the margin and in total on the group's income than votes in the larger house, h. The resulting relationship between expenditures and income (panel III) in the two chambers depends upon the relative magnitudes of the effect of expenditures on votes and the effect of votes on income in the two houses of the legislature. By construction the effect of votes on income in the senate dominates the effect of expenditures on votes in the house, so that, on net, expenditures in the senate have a more profound effect on income (margin and total) than do expenditures in the house.

In Figure 3–3 we see graphically the solution to equations (3–6) and (3–7). The optimal levels of spending in the smaller and larger houses are $(E^s)^*$ and $(E^h)^*$. From the previous discussion we know that the marginal impact of expenditures on income through votes ($Y_1V_1^h$ and $Y_1V_1^s$) is everywhere less in the house than in the senate, and we thus observe that $(E^s)^* > (E^h)^*$.

Comparative Statics

As we noted in the presentation of the model, legislative size plays an important and complex role in the lobbying process. To understand this aspect of our analysis more fully, we now explore the response of an interest group to changes in the size of the legislature and changes in the ratio of house sizes (holding total legislative size constant).

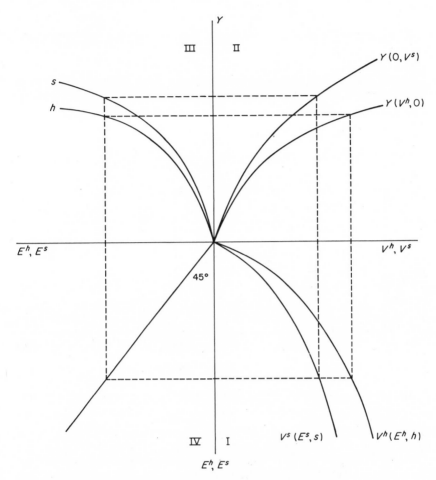

Figure 3–2. Lobbying Expenditures, Votes, and Influence

More specifically, we want to know what happens to lobbying expenditures, the amount of influence obtained from these expenditures, and the change in an interest group's net income from lobbying in the presence of these two types of changes in the size of the legislature.

To examine the effects on E^h, E^s, V, and Y_n when the total size of the legislature changes, we displace equilibrium in our model by taking

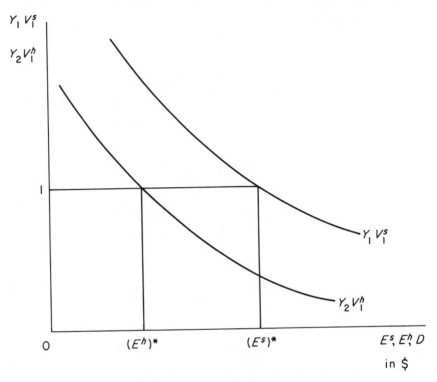

Figure 3–3. Optimal Lobbying Expenditures

the total differential of equations (3–6) and (3–7). For simplicity we will only change the size of the lower house; that is, we set $ds = 0$.

$$\frac{\partial E^h}{\partial h} = \frac{1}{|H|} \cdot \{V_1^h V_2^h (V_1^s)^2[(Y_{12})^2 - Y_{11}Y_{22}]$$

$$+ V_1^h (V_1^s)^2[Y_{12}Y_{23} - Y_{22}Y_{13}] - (V_1^s)^2 V_{12}^h Y_1 Y_{22}$$

$$- V_1^h V_2^h V_{11}^s Y_2 Y_{11} - V_1^h V_{11}^s Y_2 Y_{13} - V_{11}^s V_{12}^h Y_1 Y_2\}, \quad (3\text{–}9)$$

where

$$|H| = (V_1^h)^2 (V_1^s)^2[Y_{11}Y_{22} - (Y_{12})^2] + (V_1^h)^2 V_{11}^s Y_2 Y_{11} + (V_1^s)^2 V_{11}^h Y_1 Y_{22}$$

$$+ V_{11}^h V_{11}^s Y_1 Y_2 > 0$$

by the second-order conditions. Since $(Y_{12})^2 - Y_{11}Y_{22}$ is assumed to be nonpositive to insure that the second-order conditions are met, we know that a larger house size reduces the interest group's house expenditures if $Y_{12}Y_{23} < Y_{22}Y_{13}$. If the effect of increasing legislative size reduces the marginal impact of influence on income equally in the two houses and if the marginal effect of influence on income diminishes more rapidly in each house than across both houses, then $Y_{22}Y_{13} > Y_{12}Y_{23}$, and larger houses will result in smaller expenditures by interest groups in the houses, that is, $\partial E^h/\partial h < 0$.

Similarly, we know that

$$\frac{\partial E^s}{\partial h} = \frac{V_1^s}{|H|} \{(V_1^h)^2(Y_{12}Y_{13} - Y_{11}Y_{23})$$
$$+ Y_1Y_{12}(V_1^hV_{12}^h - V_2^hV_{11}^h) - V_{11}^hY_1Y_{23}\}. \qquad (3\text{--}10)$$

Recalling that $Y_{11}Y_{23} > Y_{12}Y_{13}$, we know from direct observation that the first and third terms in brackets in equation (3–10), including their signs, are negative. We can also show that $V_1^hV_{12}^h - V_2^hV_{11}^h > 0$ and that the second term in brackets in equation (3–10) is also negative.[7] Consequently, the interest group will also reduce its expenditures in the senate when the house size increases. Moreover, the interest group will decrease its expenditures on influence buying in the face of an increase in legislative size since its expenditures in both chambers decrease under these conditions.

Finally, we can deduce the effect of an increase in the size of the house on the net income of the interest group. Since $Y_n = Y - E$,

$$\frac{\partial Y_n}{\partial h} = \frac{\partial E^h}{\partial h}(Y_1V_1^h - 1) + \frac{\partial E^s}{\partial h}(Y_2V_1^s - 1) + Y_1V_2^h + Y_3.$$

By the first-order conditions, both $Y_1V_1^h$ and $Y_2V_1^s$ are equal to one at the optimizing level of expenditure. Hence, $\partial Y_n/\partial h = Y_1V_2^h + Y_3$, and the interest group's net income will fall if the income effect of the decline in relative influence exceeds the gain in value due to cheaper influence. Our conjecture is that the former effect dominates and that the interest group's net income falls under these conditions.

Moreover, the change in influence for an increase in house size is $\partial V/\partial h = V_1^h(\partial E^h/\partial h) + V_2^h + V_1^s(\partial E^s/\partial h)$. The effect of house size on influence thus depends upon the magnitudes of the relevant variables, even though the lobby group has spent less money; for example, where the impact of size on the price of influence is small (i.e., V_2^h is near zero), $\partial V/\partial h < 0$ and increasing house size will reduce the total influence obtained by an interest group. On the other hand if the marginal impact of lobbying expenditures on votes in the two chambers is sufficiently small as compared with the effect of size on the price of influence in the house, then the total votes obtained will increase as house size grows.

Again, the reader might consider the limiting case where all voters belong to the house (i.e., referenda for state legislation). There would seem to be no doubt in this case that milk lobbyists, for example, would have a tougher time collecting rents from price supports under referenda voting. In this case it is clear that V_2^h is near zero, and hence, the amount of influence obtained will also go down as house size increases.

In sum, then, there are some good reasons to believe that as house size increases, expenditures by the lobbying group go down, and the amount of influence obtained from these expenditures also falls (i.e., V_2^h is close to zero and $\partial V/\partial h < 0$).

A second set of relevant exercises in comparative statics deals with the effects of a change in the ratio of house sizes on the interest group's expenditures in the two houses, the influence obtained from these expenditures, and the net income of the interest group from legislation. In deriving these results, we will set $\partial s/\partial h = -1$ to avoid the confounding effect of a simultaneous increase in the total number of legislators and an overall lower price of votes.

We again employ Cramer's rule as follows to obtain the effect on expenditures in the house, since house size increases at the expense of senate size:

$$\left.\frac{\partial E^h}{\partial h}\right|_{\partial s/\partial h = -1} = \left\{\frac{1}{|H|}\right\} \cdot \{V_1^h(V_1^s)^2 V_2^h[(Y_{12})^2 - Y_{11}Y_{22}]$$

$$+ V_1^h V_{11}^s Y_2(V_2^s Y_{12} - V_2^h Y_{11}) - V_{11}^s V_{12}^h Y_1 Y_2$$

$$- V_1^h V_1^s V_{12}^s Y_2 Y_{12} - V_{12}^h (V_1^s)^2 Y_1 Y_{22}\}.$$

If we assume that the diminishing returns of votes to income within each house are the same as the diminishing returns of votes to income across both houses (i.e., that $Y_{11} = Y_{12} = Y_{22}$), then expenditures in the house will decrease when the house to senate ratio increases; that is,

$$\left.\frac{\partial E^h}{\partial h}\right|_{\partial s/\partial h = -1} = - V_{11}^s V_{12}^h Y_1 Y_2 - V_1^h V_1^s V_{12}^s Y_2 Y_{12} - V_{12}^h (V_1^s)^2 Y_1 Y_{22} < 0.$$

Analogously, the effect on expenditures in the senate as house size is increased at the expense of senate size is

$$\left.\frac{\partial E^s}{\partial h}\right|_{\partial s/\partial h = -1} = \left\{\frac{1}{|H|}\right\} \cdot \{(V_1^h)^2 V_1^s V_2^s [Y_{11} Y_{22} - (Y_{12})^2]$$

$$+ V_1^s V_{11}^h Y_1 [V_2^s Y_{22} - V_2^h Y_{12}] + (V_1^h)^2 V_{12}^s Y_2 Y_{11}$$

$$+ V_{11}^h V_{12}^s Y_1 Y_2 + V_1^h V_1^s V_{12}^h Y_1 Y_{12}\}.$$

Again, if $Y_{12} = Y_{11} = Y_{22}$, increasing the house to senate ratio will increase the interest group's expenditures in the senate because

$$\left.\frac{\partial E^s}{\partial h}\right|_{\partial s/\partial h = -1} = (V_1^h)^2 V_{12}^s Y_2 Y_{11} + V_{11}^h V_{12}^s Y_1 Y_2 + V_1^h V_1^s V_{12}^h Y_1 Y_{12} > 0.$$

It should be noted that the assumption of the equality of diminishing returns of votes to income within and across houses is a sufficient, but not necessary, condition for house expenditures to fall and senate expenditures to rise when the ratio of house to senate size increases. If the diminishing returns of votes to income are not equal, the results are ambiguous and depend upon the relative magnitudes of the variables.

Consider next what happens to the total number of votes that the interest group's expenditures win with an increase in h at the expense of s. The change in V for the parametric change in house to senate size is given by

$$\left.\frac{\partial V}{\partial h}\right|_{\partial s/\partial h = -1} = V_1^h \left.\frac{\partial E^h}{\partial h}\right|_{\partial s/\partial h = -1} + V_2^h + V_1^s \left.\frac{\partial E^s}{\partial h}\right|_{\partial s/\partial h = -1} - V_2^s.$$

If $Y_{11} = Y_{12} = Y_{22}$, then

$$\left.\frac{\partial V}{\partial h}\right|_{\partial s/\partial h = -1} = \left[\frac{Y_1 Y_2 (V_{11}^h V_1^s V_{12}^s - V_1^h V_{12}^h V_{11}^s)}{|H|}\right] + V_2^h - V_2^s. \quad (3\text{-}11)$$

Since $s < h$, increases in s should have a greater impact on the price of influence than equal increases in h and a greater impact on votes, or $V_2^h - V_2^s < 0$. Then if the ratio of the marginal products of expenditures (to votes) is greater than the ratio at which they diminish, weighted by the ratio of the marginal impact of chamber size to marginal product of expenditures (i.e., $V_{11}^h V_1^s V_{12}^s < V_1^h V_{12}^h V_{11}^s$), we know that the total influence obtained will decrease if the house to senate ratio increases. Otherwise, it again becomes a question of the relative magnitudes of the variables.

Finally, the change in the lobby's return from seeking legislation is

$$\frac{\partial Y_n}{\partial h}\bigg|_{\partial s/\partial h = -1} = \frac{\partial E^h}{\partial h}\bigg|_{\partial s/\partial h = -1} (Y_1 V_1^h - 1) + \frac{\partial E^s}{\partial h}\bigg|_{\partial s/\partial h = -1} (Y_2 V_1^s - 1)$$
$$+ Y_1 V_2^h - Y_2 V_2^s.$$

We know that $Y_1 V_1^h = Y_2 V_1^s = 1$, and hence

$$\frac{\partial Y_n}{\partial h}\bigg|_{\partial s/\partial h = -1} = Y_1 V_2^h - Y_2 V_2^s \gtreqless 0,$$

as

$$\frac{Y_1}{Y_2} \gtreqless \frac{V_2^s}{V_2^h}. \tag{3-12}$$

Equation (3-12) is not strictly determinate. Since we have assumed that $V_2^s > V_2^h$ and $h > s$ and since it is quite plausible that at the optimizing level of expenditures, the marginal impact on income of senate influence is at least as large as the marginal impact of house influence on income (i.e., $Y_2 \geq Y_1$), we believe that

$$\frac{\partial Y_n}{\partial h}\bigg|_{\partial s/\partial h = -1} < 0.$$

The Effect of Group Size

A more complicated version of our model formally incorporates the role of group size into the rent-seeking calculus of the special-interest group. Suppose that the interest group has the prerogative to control the number of its members. The group is thereby faced in our analytics with the problem of selecting not only its level of lobbying expenditure but also the income-maximizing group size. In this context group size is a two-edged sword. Increasing group size over small sizes offers the opportunity for the group to provide increased support for politicians, as the costs of preventing free riding are low, a condition that reduces the costs of influence or votes to the group. But the returns from increasing group size diminish rapidly as free riding by group members (e.g., not voting) becomes increasingly expensive to prevent.

In our basic model of income maximization by an interest group, as given in equations (3-1) through (3-5), a modification to include considerations of group size occurs in the original equations (3–4) and (3–5). The new specifications are

$$V^h = V^h(E^h, h, N) \qquad (3\text{-}4')$$

and

$$V^s = V^s(E^s, s, N), \qquad (3\text{-}5')$$

where N is the number of members in the interest group. Once again, we maximize the group's net income, as given in equation (3–1), by inserting equations (3–2) through (3–5) into equation (3–1), but now the group's choice variables are E^h, E^s, and N. The necessary conditions for a maximum are $Y_1 V_1^h = 1$; $Y_2 V_1^s = 1$; and $(V_3^h/V_3^s) = (Y_2/Y_1)$.

By assuming that both V_{33}^h and V_{33}^s are nonpositive, we know that income is concave in lobby size as

$$\left. \frac{\partial^2 Y}{\partial L^2} \right|_{V^s = 0} = Y_1 V_{33}^h + (V_3^h)^2 Y_{11} < 0$$

and

$$\left. \frac{\partial^2 Y}{\partial L^2} \right|_{V^h = 0} = Y_2 V_{33}^s + (V_3^s)^2 Y_{22} < 0.$$

V_{33}^s and V_{33}^h are zero in the range of group sizes where free riding no longer influences the political support or participation of the group's membership. In this range, for example, some absolute minimum number of group members, who vote for reasons other than their interest-group's concern (e.g., consumption), will support particular politicians, albeit at a lower level, and thereby reduce the cost of special-interest legislation to their group. Thus ever increasing group size beyond some point maps into asymptotic voter support for politicians at election time and therefore into a constant level of influence from politicians in support of the group.

It should be stressed that the optimal group size will vary considerably among interest groups. Numerous factors will work to influence the level of free riding, that is, $V^h(0, h^0, N)$ and $V^s(0, s^0, N)$. As the group improves its ability to control free riding, the functions $V^h(\cdot)$, $V^s(\cdot)$, $V_3^h(\cdot)$, and $V_3^s(\cdot)$ will all shift upward and improve the marginal productivity of vote buying.

The purpose of analyzing the effects of group size, outside of an intrinsic interest in its own right, is twofold. First, an equilibrium in this market will generate zero returns at the intensive and extensive margins. Small groups and groups with uncommon abilities to control free riding should enjoy inframarginal gains relative to the market but zero returns at their own margin. Larger groups (the entire polity in the limit) will likely find that even inframarginal returns are low or zero, because their vote production functions are low and flat due to the fact that they offer little in the way of support for politicians. Second, we note that it is not necessarily an implication of the theory of economic regulation that successful interest groups are small. Our analysis here demonstrates that this is not necessarily the case. Consider that interest groups can offer politicians both dollars and votes in return for political favors. Politicians can convert votes into dollars through reduced campaign expenditures and higher present values of their seats. This implies that an interest group need not be small to be successful in receiving transfers from the state but they must be capable of preventing free riding.

A Majoritarian Interpretation of the Model

As we noted at the outset of our analysis, we have heretofore been using votes in the broad sense of influence rather than in the strict sense of one man–one vote. What happens if we suppose that the success of an interest group is based upon whether it achieves a simple majority of the legislators in each house? In this case we can easily show that if $V^h(\tilde{E}, h^0)$ is equal to $V^s(\tilde{E}, s^0)$, where $h^0 = s^0$, the total vote obtained by a lobbyist will be maximized for any given level of expenditures, $\tilde{E}$, if the two chambers are of equal size.[8]

Consider a legislature of 100 members equally divided between house and senate. A simple majority voting rule dictates that twenty-six votes in each house are required for legislative success. Suppose that winning those fifty-two votes costs E^* dollars. Compare E^* with the cost of winning a simple majority where the 100 legislators are divided into sixty-six representatives and thirty-four senators. If the costs of making collective decisions increase at an increasing rate, the extra cost of convincing eight more votes in the house will exceed the saving from buying eight less votes in the senate, and the total expense, $\hat{E}$, of obtaining fifty-two votes in this fashion will exceed E^*, the cost when the legislators were equally divided between house and senate. An important principle thus emerges — interest groups will be most successful where the two houses of a bicameral legislature are of equal size, ceteris paribus.

Testable Implications

There are essentially four testable implications of this theory of lobbying. First, interest groups will fare better in the market for legislation where the two houses of the legislature are more equal in size. Second, larger legislatures will frustrate the rent-seeking activities of interest groups. Third, wealthier jurisdictions will exhibit more rent seeking. Fourth, a larger population will induce more rent seeking. We now turn to the presentation of some empirical tests that do not refute these implications of the theory.

EMPIRICAL EVIDENCE FROM STATE LEGISLATURES

The major empirical implications of our analysis concern the effects of a bicameral vote market on the returns from lobbying. We expect that where the ratio of house to senate size is lower and where the overall size of the legislature is smaller, the rate of return to interest groups from lobbying will be higher. In this section we present two sets of evidence that are consistent with these implications of the theory.

The Degree of Economic Regulation across States

If one subscribes to the major findings of theory of economic regulation, then a reasonable proxy for the success of interest groups would be the degree of economic regulation qua monopoly across states; in other words, the level of economic regulation, as measured, for example, by the amount of enforcement activity, is one possible measure of the level of monopoly privileges granted by a legislature, ostensibly in response to lobbying activity. If our theory holds water, the level of enforcement activity will be predictably related to the ratio of house sizes, legislative size, wealth, and population across states.[9] For the reader's inspection Table 3–1 reports the "protective regulation" expenses of each state and the sizes of the respective legislative houses.

Table 3-1. Protective Inspection and Regulation Expenses (thousands) and House and Senate Size by State, 1975

State	Expenses ($)	House Members	Senate Members
Alabama	10,723	105	35
Alaska	5,291	40	20
Arizona	12,813	60	30
Arkansas	6,878	100	35
California	142,671	80	40
Colorado	9,121	65	35
Connecticut	15,527	151	36
Delaware	2,418	41	21
Florida	40,081	120	40
Georgia	11,183	180	56
Hawaii	4,693	51	25
Idaho	5,190	70	35
Illinois	49,211	177	59
Indiana	11,152	100	50
Iowa	12,157	100	50
Kansas	7,561	125	40
Kentucky	14,582	100	38
Louisiana	16,480	105	39
Maine	5,018	151	33
Maryland	18,609	141	47
Massachusetts	22,923	240	40
Michigan	34,182	110	38
Minnesota	13,849	134	67
Mississippi	11,561	122	52
Missouri	16,159	163	34
Montana	3,878	100	50
Nebraska	8,671	—	49
Nevada	6,336	40	20
New Hampshire	3,939	400	24
New Jersey	42,691	80	40
New Mexico	4,878	70	42
New York	148,785	150	60
North Carolina	19,519	120	50
North Dakota	3,635	100	50
Ohio	36,205	99	33
Oklahoma	8,848	101	48
Oregon	11,310	60	30
Pennsylvania	39,803	203	50

Table 3–1 — *continued*

State	Expenses ($)	House Members	Senate Members
Rhode Island	3,674	100	50
South Carolina	12,469	124	46
South Dakota	3,537	70	35
Tennessee	13,227	99	33
Texas	40,954	150	31
Utah	5,965	75	29
Vermont	3,754	150	30
Virginia	22,463	100	40
Washington	25,932	98	49
West Virginia	7,922	100	34
Wisconsin	19,015	99	33
Wyoming	1,483	62	30

SOURCE: U.S. Department of Commerce, Bureau of the Census, *State Government Finances* (Washington, D.C.: Government Printing Office, 1976); and Council of State Governments, *Book of the States, 1976–1977* (Lexington, Ky.: Iron Works Pike, 1976).

To test these implications of our theory we estimated four versions of the following model:

$$REG = a_0 + a_1(RATIO) + a_2(ASSOC) + a_3(YPC) + a_4(RPC)$$
$$+ a_5(SPC) + a_6(POP) + a_7(POP^2) + a_8(SIZE) + \mu,$$

where

REG = protective inspection and regulation expenses;
$RATIO$ = ratio of house to senate size;
$ASSOC$ = number of trade associations;
YPC = per capita state personal income;
RPC = number of representatives per capita;
SPC = number of senators per capita;
POP = state population;
$SIZE$ = size of legislature;
μ = a random error term.

The results of estimating four specifications of this model by ordinary least squares are reported in Table 3–2.[10]

Table 3-2. Regression Results for Protective Inspection and Regulation Expenses, 1975

Explanatory Variable	Coefficient/t-statistic			
Constant	-643.98	11285.5	8059.7	11809.5
	(-0.07)	(2.03)**	(0.88)	(1.91)**
ASSOC	18.27	15.92	20.60	16.1
	(5.03)***	(6.92)***	(5.73)***	(6.41)***
RATIO	-4617.7	-2238.4	-2057.7	-2086.3
	(-2.92)***	(-2.24)**	(-1.11)	(-1.66)*
YPC	10116.8	9041.2	1687.9	8576.0
	(0.66)	(0.93)	(0.11)	(0.85)
RPC	151136	65148	123392	63440
	(2.82)***	(1.93)**	(2.36)**	(1.81)**
SPC	-232075	-27794	-178364	-27522
	(-1.50)*	(-2.83)***	(-1.20)	(-2.75)***
POP	5.0		5.09	
	(11.1)***		(11.78)***	
(POP^2)		0.26×10^{-6}		0.26×10^{-6}
		(19.1)***		(18.8)***
SIZE			-80.4	-4.71
			(-2.36)**	(-0.20)
R^2	0.93	0.97	0.94	0.97
F-statistic	96.6***	249.1***	92.3***	208.7***

SOURCE: See note 10.
NOTE: * — significant at the 10 percent level; ** — significant at the 5 percent level; *** — significant at the 1 percent level.

We observe strong support for the proposition that the level of economic regulation across states is related negatively to the disparity in house sizes. In all specifications the coefficient on *RATIO* is negative, and it is significant in each case except the specification where *SIZE* appears without population squared. The latter result is most likely the result of the rather high correlation between *SIZE* and *RATIO* (0.80), which acts to reduce the t-statistics on both variables. The coefficient on *SIZE* is also negative, being significant in one specification but not in the other. Moreover, the pattern of results on the other independent variables is generally consistent with our analysis. As we hypothesized, population plays an important role in the determination of the level of economic regulation in all the specifications. The wealth of a state is proxied by income per capita, and in all specifications we obtain positive but insignificant signs. Moreover, as one might reasonably expect, the number of trade associations is positively and significantly related to the measure of economic regulation.[11]

Two additional remarks about these results are relevant. First, if the reader is concerned that the total amount of regulation is the wrong way to measure monopoly power across states, our results are consistent if we define the dependent variable in per capita terms (*REG/POP*). The coefficients show the predicted signs at comparable levels of significance in such a specification, though we obtain a smaller R^2 as one might reasonably expect. Second, there may be some concern that the number of trade associations is a product of a fertile breeding ground (e.g., a low *RATIO* and a low *SIZE*), and *ASSOC* is therefore endogenous to the model. A two-equation estimation yields the same results cited here.

The Degree of Occupational Regulation across States

Occupational licensing is a specific and important manifestation of the theory of economic regulation. Few careful observers would disagree that the benefits of licensing accrue to members of the licensed profession in the form of increased rents due to entry limitations and restrictions on price competition within the profession. Moreover, such legislation typically results from lobbying pressure by practitioners in the occupation; for example, "The sponsoring group usually drafts the legislation and then has it introduced by a friendly legislator. Members and friends participate in an organized letter-writing campaign to support the legislation; practitioners and paid lobbyists call on legislators in person to obtain commitments for the law."[12] If the size of the legislature and the ratio of house sizes are important to the success of lobbying, then the number of licensed occupations in a state ought to be sensitive to such variables.

As an important additional test of the theory of lobbying, we therefore propose to examine whether states with larger legislatures and higher ratios of house to senate size are characterized by less successful lobbying for occupational licensing. Moreover, the data for this additional empirical work are based upon a 1952 cross-section of forty-eight state legislatures and the occupations licensed by each state. Applying the theory to explain the extent of occupational licensing in this period presents a challenge in two senses. First, there is not a large variation to be explained in the 1952 data on the number of occupations licensed across states, as reported in Table 3–3. Arizona and Utah licensed twenty-eight occupations (the most), and Mississippi eighteen (the least). Indeed, it must be kept in mind throughout our empirical work that competition among these highly open state jurisdictions will lead to substantial uniformity in monopoly power across states and that we have in general selected a difficult cross-sectional basis for testing our theory. Second, checking the explanatory power of the theory on data from an earlier period should give some idea of the robustness of the model.[13]

Since there is a high statistical correlation between size of the legislature and the ratio of house sizes in the 1952 data (0.81), we report the results of estimating three specifications of the following model:

$$LIC = b_0 + b_1(Y) + b_2(DEN) + b_3(PROFARM) + b_4(SIZE)$$
$$+ b_5(RATIO) + \mu,$$

where

LIC = natural log of the number of licensed occupations per state;

Y = state personal income;

DEN = state population density;

$PROFARM$ = proportion of the state population employed in agriculture;

$SIZE$ = size of state legislature;

$RATIO$ = ratio of house to senate size;

μ = a random error term.

Table 3–3. Occupations Licensed by the State and Legislative Size, 1952

State	Total No. of Occupations Licensed	House Size	Senate Size
Alabama	20	106	35
Arizona	28	80	19
Arkansas	23	100	35
California	27	80	40
Colorado	22	65	35
Connecticut	25	279	36
Delaware	23	35	17
Florida	27	95	38
Georgia	26	205	54
Idaho	24	59	44
Illinois	27	153	51
Indiana	24	100	50
Iowa	24	108	50
Kansas	24	125	40
Kentucky	24	100	38
Louisiana	26	100	39
Maine	22	151	33
Maryland	25	123	29
Massachusetts	20	240	40
Michigan	24	100	32
Minnesota	23	131	67
Mississippi	18	140	49
Missouri	19	157	34
Montana	22	94	56
Nebraska	20	—	43
Nevada	20	47	17
New Hampshire	21	400	24
New Jersey	26	60	21
New Mexico	24	55	31
New York	25	150	56
North Carolina	26	120	50
North Dakota	25	113	49
Ohio	25	136	33
Oklahoma	25	118	44
Oregon	26	60	30
Pennsylvania	23	208	50
Rhode Island	23	100	40
South Carolina	24	124	46

Table 3–3 — continued

State	Total No. of Occupations Licensed	House Size	Senate Size
South Dakota	21	75	35
Tennessee	23	99	33
Texas	25	150	31
Utah	28	60	23
Vermont	22	246	30
Virginia	25	100	40
Washington	25	99	46
West Virginia	20	100	32
Wisconsin	26	100	33
Wyoming	24	56	27

SOURCE: Council of State Governments, *Occupational Licensing in the States* (Chicago: Council of State Governments, 1952).

The results of estimating this model by ordinary least squares are given in Table 3–4.[14]

When entered alone, both *RATIO* and *SIZE* are negative and significantly different from zero at the 5 percent level. These highly related characteristics of legislatures thus continue to be important predictors of lobbying success. When entered together, both are negative but not statistically significant, a result possibly due to their high simple correlation.[15] State personal income, population density, and the proportion of farm workers account for cross-sectional differences in state wealth, the potential supply of wealth transfers, and economic homogeneity. In each case we find the expected sign. Higher state income or wealth is associated with greater lobbying success, that is, more licensed occupations.[16] Higher population densities frustrate lobbying because the suppliers of wealth transfers find it less costly to defeat special-interest legislation where they can more easily associate physically with one another.[17] In states where the proportion of the population employed in agriculture is large, occupations are less successful in obtaining licensing legislation, a not so surprising result since the extent of agriculture is a proxy for the degree of homogeneous interest in a population.[18]

Table 3–4. Regression Results for Occupations Licensed by the States, 1952

Explanatory Variable	Coefficient/t-statistic		
Constant	3.25	3.25	3.25
	(66.4)***	(66.0)***	(64.81)***
Y	0.29×10^{-13}	0.41×10^{-13}	0.32×10^{-13}
	(1.21)	(1.75)**	(1.17)
DEN	−0.12	−0.09	−0.11
	(−1.12)	(−0.86)	(−1.01)
PROFARM	−1.33	−0.92	−1.24
	(−1.89)**	(−1.37)*	(−1.57)*
SIZE		-0.38×10^{-3}	-0.98×10^{-4}
		(−1.78)**	(−0.23)
RATIO	−0.012		-0.96×10^{-2}
	(−1.95)**		(−0.78)
R^2	0.19	0.18	.20
F-statistic	2.48*	2.31*	1.95

SOURCE: See note 14.
NOTE: * — significant at the 10 percent level; ** — significant at the 5 percent level; *** — significant at the 1 percent level.

Bills Enacted

We turn finally to a study of legislative enactments to shed some further evidence on the relationship between the costs of lobbying and the legislative activity of interest groups. Table 3–5 lists the bills enacted by each state legislature during the 1973–74 legislative sessions. As before, we expect h/s to be negative, whether it proxies the costs of obtaining legislation for the general-interest lobbyist or whether it proxies the same costs for the special-interest lobbyist who will be trying to procure the passage of a bill favored by his interest group.

We estimate several versions of the following model:

$$BE = c_0 + c_1 \left(\frac{h}{s}\right) + c_2(MAJ) + c_3(Y) + c_4 \left(\frac{h + s}{COMM}\right)$$

$$+ c_5(h + s) + c_6(RTEN) + c_7(POP) + c_8 \left(\frac{Y}{POP}\right) + \mu,$$

Table 3–5.   Bills Introduced and Enacted by State, 1976

State	No. of Bills Enacted	State	No. of Bills Enacted
Alabama	1,061	Montana	949
Alaska	238	Nebraska	633
Arizona	389	Nevada	810
Arkansas	894	New Hampshire	557
California	2,761	New Jersey	890
Colorado	569	New Mexico	496
Connecticut	1,286	New York	2,119
Delaware	562	North Carolina	1,482
Florida	1,287	North Dakota	516
Georgia	1,380	Ohio	403
Hawaii	476	Oklahoma	592
Idaho	673	Oregon	841
Illinois	1,297	Pennsylvania	658
Indiana	490	Rhode Island	784
Iowa	591	South Carolina	1,488
Kansas	861	South Dakota	732
Kentucky	386	Tennessee	1,196
Louisiana	1,547	Texas	688
Maine	860	Utah	254
Maryland	1,781	Vermont	276
Massachusetts	2,092	Virginia	1,388
Michigan	595	Washington	631
Minnesota	1,366	West Virginia	298
Mississippi	1,390	Wisconsin	341
Missouri	357	Wyoming	276

SOURCE: Council of State Governments, *Book of the States, 1976–1977.*

where the previously undefined variables are

BE = bills enacted;
MAJ = percentage of the majority party;
$COMM$ = sum of house, senate, and joint committees;
$RTEN$ = house term-length divided by senate term-length;

$$\frac{Y}{POP}$$ = state personal income per capita.

The results of estimating the bills-enacted equation by ordinary least squares are presented in Table 3–6 and are explained below.[19]

Primarily, we find in each specification a very powerful negative sign on h/s. This result indicates that as the costs of lobbying rise for both the general- and special-interest lobbyist, they are able to secure the passage of fewer bills through their efforts. We take this result as further strong evidence in favor of our theory. The other results in Table 3–6 are also of interest. In the context of the passage of general-interest legislation, the size of the majority variable is strongly positive, reflecting the fact that the passage of such legislation is less costly where there is a greater underlying consensus on what the general interest is. The strong positive sign on the state personal income variable mostly reflects the fact that public goods are normal goods. The measure of the number of legislators per committee, $(h + s)/COMM$, is a cost variable designed to capture the degree of legislator specialization across states. As this ratio rises, each committee member can specialize more intensively within a given area of legislative inquiry, a condition that leads to more legislation. Transaction costs of reaching committee decisions also increase as $(h + s)/COMM$ increases, a condition that suggests a countervailing effect to the specialization effect on legislative output. However, these costs can be controlled to some extent through the proliferation of subcommittees, and we thus expect the specialization effect to dominate in the data. Finally, since house terms are always less than or equal to senate terms, $RTEN$ ranges between 0 and 1. This ratio is analogous to h/s, in that as the two houses become more similar, special and general interests will face less disparity of opinion between the two houses on legislation and thereby lower costs of lobbying. As the ratio tends toward unity, we therefore expect more legislative output, an expectation that is strongly verified in the data.[20]

SUMMARY

In this chapter we proposed a testable economic theory of the behavior of an interest group in lobbying a legislature for wealth transfers. Our basic argument was that certain constitutional aspects of the legislature, primarily its size and the ratio of chamber sizes, will predictably affect the rate of return that interest groups earn from legislation. Our

Table 3–6. Bills Enacted by the State Legislatures, 1973–74

Explanatory Variable	Coefficient/t-statistic					
Intercept	-445.50	-428.995	-465.304	-501.656	-501.00	-533.453
	(-1.88)*	(-1.71)*	(-1.93)*	(-2.08)*	(-1.97)*	(-2.18)*
RATIO	-71.89		-93.32	-64.81		-91.72
	(-2.53)**		(-2.19)**	(-2.25)**		(-2.16)**
MAJ	7.75	8.64	7.41	9.97	11.089	9.77
	(2.36)**	(2.52)**	(2.22)**	(2.66)**	(2.86)**	(2.59)**
Y	0.014	0.015	0.013	0.042	0.048	0.044
	(6.43)**	(6.10)**	(5.17)**	(1.79)**	(1.93)**	(1.86)**
h + s/COMM	66.875	60.64	60.11	61.93	52.81	52.64
	(2.96)**	(2.34)**	(2.42)**	(2.71)**	(2.00)**	(2.08)**
h + s	-1.68	-1.68	1.19		-1.26	1.54
	(-1.36)*	(-1.36)*	(0.68)		(-1.00)	(0.87)
RTEN	540.46	502.50	513.36	485.16	430.11	444.08
	(2.22)**	(1.95)*	(2.07)**	(1.97)*	(1.64)*	(1.77)*
POP				-1.53×10^{-4}	-1.78×10^{-4}	-1.70×10^{-4}
				(-1.20)	(-1.32)*	(-1.31)*
R^2	0.60	0.56	0.61	0.62	0.58	0.62
F-statistic	13.37**	11.37**	11.08**	11.49**	9.92**	9.90**

SOURCE: See note 19.
NOTE: * — significant at the 5 percent level; ** — significant at the 1 percent level.

major conclusions, strongly supported by several empirical tests, were that more equal chamber sizes and smaller legislatures favor the activities of interest groups in capturing and sustaining rents by means of the political process.

NOTES

1. Here and subsequently in this chapter, we are speaking in terms of a rate of return to the interest group and not to society.

2. George J. Stigler, "Economic Competition and Political Competition," *Public Choice* 13 (Fall 1972):91–106.

3. This theory does not depend upon a monolithic idea of legislators as vote sellers. Lobbying frequently conveys information to legislators, for example, about the proportion of voters who favor or oppose a particular proposal. Thus, based upon personal convictions, attitudes toward risk, reelection prospects, and so forth, various legislators will have different Marshallian "convincing prices." What this means is that there is an ordered array of prices of influence facing the interest group, and for analytical simplicity we simply assume that all influence is purchased.

4. See Eugene F. Fama and Arthur B. Laffer, "The Number of Firms and Competition," *American Economic Review* 62 (September 1972):670–74.

5. Consider the following example of this discussion: A firm wins the influence of one legislator out of fifty. Facing a six-month delay in obtaining permission from the environmental board to discharge a certain amount of waste, the firm requests that the legislator phone the board. The delay is reduced to two months at the legislator's insistence.

Now consider the same example where there are seventy-five legislators. The environmental board will be less concerned about the request of any one legislator because there are more of them, each with proportionately less control over the activities of the agency, and the legislator's phone call will be worth less under these circumstances.

The moral of the story is that only by increasing relative influence can income from lobbying be increased.

6. The second-order conditions sufficient to guarantee a maximum of equation (3–1) are

$$(V_1^h)^2 Y_{11} + Y_1 V_{11}^h < 0,$$

which is satisfied by an assumption of diminishing returns of votes to income and of expenditures to votes, and

$$(V_1^h)^2 (V_1^s)^2 [Y_{11} Y_{22} - (Y_{12})^2] + Y_{11} Y_2 V_{11}^s (V_1^h)^2 + Y_1 V_{11}^h Y_{22} (V_1^s)^2 + Y_1 Y_2 V_{11}^h V_{11}^s > 0.$$

A sufficient but not necessary condition for this is that $Y_{11}Y_{22} \geq (Y_{12})^2$. This condition will hold if diminishing returns of votes on income within each house are at least as large as the diminishing returns of votes on income across both houses taken together. We maintain such an assumption in the subsequent analysis.

7. Visualize a production mountain of votes depending upon house size and lobbying expenditures. The iso-vote curve in this map will be convex because V_1^h and V_2^h are both positive and because V_{11}^h and V_{22}^h are negative. The slope of these iso-vote curves is $-(V_1^h/V_2^h)$. The rate of change of the slope as we increase E^h holding h constant is

$$\frac{\partial(-V_1^h/V_2^h)}{\partial E^h} = -\frac{V_{11}^h V_2^h - V_{12}^h V_1^h}{(V_2^h)^2}.$$

If V^h is linearly homogeneous in E^h and h or is homothetic, the slopes of the iso-vote functions are less negatively sloped as we increase E^h holding h constant. It then follows clearly that $V_1^h V_{12}^h - V_2^h V_{11}^h > 0$.

8. Simply maximize V subject to $h + s = a$ constant, and observe that $V_2^h(\cdot) = V_2^s(\cdot)$ is a necessary condition that will hold only if $s = h$. Other institutional characteristics of the two houses, such as term lengths, will obviously affect the application of this result. Our assertion here holds to the extent that these other characteristics are approximately the same in both houses. The second-order conditions are guaranteed by the assumption of diminishing returns of chamber size to votes, that is, that both V_{22}^s and V_{22}^h are negative.

9. For the reader's inspection, the correlation matrix for the independent variables in our first empirical test is given here. Variable definitions and data sources appear later in the text.

	ASSOC	YPC	SIZE	Y	RPC	SPC	POP	RATIO
ASSOC	1.0							
YPC	0.30	1.0						
SIZE	0.24	−0.16	1.0					
Y	0.75	0.32	0.23	1.0				
RPC	−0.21	−0.18	0.42	−0.40	1.0			
SPC	−0.31	−0.02	−0.25	−0.57	0.60	1.0		
POP	0.71	0.24	0.25	0.99	−0.42	−0.60	1.0	
RATIO	−0.02	−0.16	.80	−0.01	0.71	−0.07	−0.001	1.0

10. The coefficients in Table 3–2 are estimated from 1975 data on U.S. states. Data sources are Council of State Governments, *Book of the States, 1976–1977* (Lexington, Ky.: Iron Works Pike, 1976); Gale Research Company, *Encyclopedia of Associations* (Detroit: Ruffner, 1973); *Statistical Abstract of the United States, 1977* (Washington, D.C.: Government Printing Office, 1977); and U.S. Department of Commerce, Bureau of the Census, *State Government Finances* (Washington, D.C.: Government Printing Office, 1976).

Estimating this model by weighted least squares, where the weighting device is the square root of population, does not appreciably change the results in Table 3–2. Nebraska's unicameral legislature presents an interesting problem for our theory; that is, special interests should be very successful in Nebraska because there is no second house in the legislature. Econometrically, we handle this problem by aligning the Nebraska legislature with state senates and by setting $h = 0$. Nonetheless, our empirical results are basically unchanged if we simply drop Nebraska.

11. Similar results are obtained if $ASSOC/POP$ is used rather than $ASSOC$.

12. B. Shimberg, B. F. Esser, and D. H. Krueger, *Occupational Licensing* (Lansing, Mich.: Educational Testing Service and Michigan State University Press, 1972), p. 14.

13. The correlation matrix for the independent variables in this second test of our theory is given here. As before, variable definitions and data sources appear later in the text.

	Y	*DEN*	*PROFARM*	*RATIO*	*SIZE*	*Y/POP*
Y	1.0					
DEN	0.32	1.0				
PROFARM	−0.40	−0.52	1.0			
RATIO	−0.04	0.12	−0.28	1.0		
SIZE	0.17	0.20	−0.13	0.80	1.0	
Y/POP	0.42	0.42	−0.65	0.03	−0.07	1.0

14. The coefficients in Table 3–4 are estimated from 1952 data on U.S. states. Data sources are Council of State Governments, *Occupational Licensing in the States* (Chicago: Council of State Governments, 1952); and *Statistical Abstract of the United States, 1953* (Washington, D.C.: Government Printing Office, 1953). As in the case of the first empirical model above, least squares estimates of this model weighted by the square root of population differ hardly at all from the results given in Table 3–4. Three further points are relevant to the estimation of the occupational licensing model. First, following George J. Stigler, "The Sizes of Legislatures," *Journal of Legal Studies* 5 (January 1976):17–34, one might be concerned that legislative size is endogenous. However, estimation of our model with Stigler's equation for legislative size yields essentially the same results as those obtained by ordinary least squares. We thus report only the latter results here. Second, logarithmic and linear specifications produce similar results. Third, while we still obtain negative signs on *SIZE* and *RATIO*, regressions of this model that incorporate *RPC* and *SPC* are not significant.

15. The sequential F-statistic on *SIZE* and *RATIO* is 1.88 and is significant at the 20 percent level.

16. We employ *Y* rather than *Y/POP* in this specification because it provides a better fit to the data. The results are basically unaltered by the use of *Y/POP*.

17. Higher density, of course, lowers the costs of organizing and controlling free riding for both winners and losers in the wealth-transfer process, but it lowers these costs *relatively* more for the losers because they face a more acute free-rider problem by definition.

18. *PROFARM* is a proxy for the extent of special-interest activity in this model. We would have preferred to use *ASSOC*, as in the regulation expenses model, but there is no data on this variable for 1952.

19. Data on the previously undefined variables in the empirical results presented in Table 3–6 are taken from *Book of the States, 1976–1977.* Also, for a related analysis, see W. Mark Crain, "Costs and Outputs in the Legislative Firm," *Journal of Legal Studies* 8 (June 1979):607–21.

20. Alternative specifications of the bills-enacted equation produce similar results; for example, using income per capita rather than income, or using population squared instead of (or with) population, or including the total number of legislative committees does not materially affect the empirical conclusions found in Table 3–6.

4 LEGISLATURES AS WAGE CARTELS

In this chapter we begin our consideration of politicians as brokers in the wealth transfer process. The first order of business in this regard is to develop some understanding of how the market for politicians functions — that is, what forms does competition take in this market? Our basic approach will be to consider politicians as participants in a labor market and to analyze the nature of competition for the legitimate returns from holding office. As we shall see, this competition has a monopolistic and a competitive variant. The question of extralegal returns in the political sector is deferred until Chapter 5.

Our explanation of legislative pay will seem familiar to economists. Nonetheless, it will contrast markedly with the explanations and approaches to the same problem offered by other expert observers of

This chapter has been reprinted from Robert E. McCormick and Robert D. Tollison, "Legislatures as Unions," *Journal of Political Economy* 86 (February 1978):63–78, by permission of The University of Chicago Press. © 1978 by The University of Chicago.

such matters. The following quotations provide a menu of competing hypotheses:

> Despite the fact that in recent years a few states have provided substantial salaries for their legislators, no public servant in relation to his responsibilities is more underpaid.
>
> Most states fail to pay their lawmakers anything approximating a living wage.
>
> To a large extent, legislators are paid according to the frequency of regular sessions.
>
> Legislators in annual session States generally fare better than lawmakers in biennial States.
>
> As many analysts have pointed out, the most significant variable in determining the size of legislative salaries appears to be state population.[1]

Our explanation of legislative pay is fueled by a completely different mental set than that implied in the initial two quotations. We also provide a more complete model of the determination of legislative pay with which the type of claims made by the last three sources can be evaluated.

In effect, we view legislators as participants in a labor market, and we try to explain differences in the legal pay of legislators by factors that affect the supply of and demand for their services. We present a model of the legislature as a labor union, whose wage is set in some states in the constitution (the analogue to competition) and in others by the legislators (monopoly). We test the implications of the model with respect to relative legislator wages in the two types of states and with respect to other aspects of the legislature as a union (e.g., size of the legislature). The implications of the model hold up quite well in empirical tests.

Basically, as we discussed in Chapter 1, we share Stigler's concern with modeling the central tasks of representation properly. He states that "the central task of representation is to give efficient representation to the collection of group interests that express the desires of citizens who compose the state."[2] We pose a corollary question, namely, what is the legal payoff to the representative for performing those tasks?

In the first section below we present a model stressing the supply of and demand for legislator services under union and nonunion conditions. The model involves the solution of a unique problem of present value maximization. In the second section we perform an empirical test of the implications of the model regarding relative legislator wages using data for 1974 on state governments. In a final section we offer some brief concluding remarks on the relation between the pay of legislators and the prospects for malfeasance.

THEORY AND PRELIMINARY IMPLICATIONS

The wide range in legislative pay among the fifty states is illustrated in Table 4–1. Biennial pay for legislators in 1974–75 ranges from $200 in New Hampshire to $64,140 in California. Stigler's remarks about the small range of variation in the size of legislatures are reversed for legislative pay. This is quite a wide range of variation in wages across states, and this paper presents an explanation of this variation.

The supply of legislative services is analogous to the supply of any service where labor is extensively used in (roughly) fixed proportions to other inputs. The quantity supplied of legislative services (which we will measure in man-years per year) is therefore determined by the relative wage, the price of inputs other than labor, and technology. Each state has a separate supply function, but we do not expect the conditions of supply to vary greatly across states. Potential legislators are never a finite fraction of the available labor in a state, and the occupational composition of legislatures is highly similar across states. These positions are held primarily by members of professions that can capitalize readily on certain aspects of being a legislator. Lawyers thereby avoid the professional ban on advertising (at least until the recent Supreme Court decision), and often continue to draw a wage from their law firms while serving. Farmers can be legislators where sessions are held between growing seasons. The reason that banking, insurance, and real estate people gravitate to these offices is not hard to discern. Our theory will lead us to expect relatively more legislators, such as lawyers, who can combine legislative service with outside earning opportunities in states where the legislative wage is low, but we defer this discussion until Chapter 5.

Table 4–1. Estimated Biennial Compensation of Legislators, 1974–75

State	Biennial Compensation ($)	State	Biennial Compensation ($)
New Hampshire	200	Georgia	18,432
Rhode Island	600	Kansas	18,928
Utah	3,200	Arizona	19,170
Wyoming	3,348	Tennessee	19,909
Arkansas	3,600	Oklahoma	19,920
New Mexico	3,600	New Jersey	20,000
Maine	4,250	Oregon	20,010
North Dakota	6,540	Delaware	21,050
Montana	6,954	Indiana	21,420
South Dakota	7,475	Iowa	21,580
Idaho	7,535	Minnesota	23,862
Nevada	8,260	Maryland	25,000
Vermont	8,430	Virginia	25,850
Nebraska	10,000	Mississippi	26,480
Washington	11,200	Florida	27,125
Kentucky	12,350	Massachusetts	27,776
West Virginia	12,600	Hawaii	28,960
Alabama	12,940	Pennsylvania	31,200
Connecticut	13,000	Wisconsin	31,356
South Carolina	14,400	Ohio	35,000
Colorado	15,200	Michigan	38,000
Missouri	16,800	Alaska	43,920
Texas	17,400	Illinois	49,424
North Carolina	17,635	New York	57,500
Louisiana	18,000	California	64,140

SOURCE: Council of State Governments, *Book of the States, 1976–1977* (Lexington, Ky.: Iron Works Pike, 1976), p. 37.

NOTE: Includes salary, daily pay, and unvouchered expense allowances. Excludes special session compensation, per diem business allowances, mileage and transportation, and all vouchered expenses. In instances in which daily pay or expenses were provided, days in session were estimated on the basis of days in session in 1973–74.

In each state there is some demand for legislative influence. The demand for legislative influence implies a derived demand for legislators. For reasons discussed in Chapter 3, the technical relationship between influence and legislators is not one of proportionality because an excessive number of legislators would dilute the influence of each and might not be able to pass any laws. We further expect that given the lack of low-cost substitutes for legislative action within a state, the elasticity of the demand for representation with respect to the legislative wage rate must be close to zero over the relevant range. Across states, in contrast to the relative invariability of supply in this market, we expect that the demand for representation will shift as a function of state income, population, budget size, and so forth.

With this background in mind, we note that wage determination takes essentially two forms among states. In some states legislative pay is set in the constitution and is quite difficult to change. A new wage would require the passage of a constitutional proposal. Such proposals typically emanate from the legislature under relatively strict voting and quorum rules and must be signed by the governor and passed in a statewide referendum. In other states, pay is set by a statute passed by both houses of the legislature and signed by the governor. These pay bills are subject to legislative consideration under normal voting and quorum rules and do not require a statewide referendum.[3]

We contend that legislative determination of pay by statute amounts to a strong form of union power. Unions typically achieve higher relative wages by restricting entry. In this case entry is somewhat more loosely controlled by means of constitutional limitations on the size of the legislature and on the procedures for gaining a seat, and legislators are given a direct hand in wage determination. We would expect to observe the impact of this monopoly power in higher relative wages for legislators in these states.

The conditions in the legislative labor market for a single state are depicted in Figure 4–1. Each legislature is treated as a separate labor market. A measure of legislative output (Q_L) in terms of man-years per year is on the horizontal axis, and annual legal pay (W_L) as dollars per man-year is on the vertical axis. The competitive supply curve for successful applicants for these seats is given by S. This relationship represents the wage that must be forthcoming for a given level of output to persuade prospective legislators to run for and to accept office. Following our previous argument, we draw a completely inelastic demand curve over the relevant range for the services of legislators. In the absence of any contrary evidence, we assume that existing wages clear the market for the given constraint on legislative size in both union and nonunion states — that is, there is no excess supply.

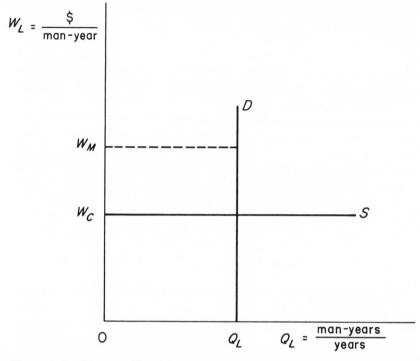

Figure 4–1.   Wages of Legislators

In states where the legislative wage is constitutionally determined, some given wage, W_C, will prevail. Candidates will adjust to the given wage, and supply or marginal opportunity costs will shift accordingly as more- or less-qualified individuals seek election, so that the market clears. In states that allow legislative control over pay, the wage is adjusted by legislators to maximize the present value of a seat. This wage is, for the moment, arbitrarily drawn in Figure 4–1 at W_M. There are no free rents in this case because higher pay will be dissipated in competition for seats. If W_M is high, more able individuals will compete for legislative seats, and in the long run they will receive a competitive rate of return by having higher opportunity costs, or by spending more to capture seats, or both. Thus, there will only be gains from unexpected increases in wage rates.

The main issue confronting this theory concerns the forces that constrain the legislator from setting an infinite wage in Figure 4–1. Since we argue that the demand for legislator time is completely inelastic over the relevant range, this pay problem reduces to a question of what limits the wage-setting ability of the legislature under these conditions.

Think of the problem in this way. Imagine that the Wish Fairy makes you the following proposition: You may make a wish today, but one year from now the fairy will return and (1) grant you your wish and allow you to make another one, or (2) deny your wish and disallow you any more wishes.[4] The fairy's decision is predicated on the premise that the higher the wish, the more likely is option 2 (rejection at the polls). The question facing the typical legislator under these conditions, then, is what wage to wish for when the wage goes into effect after the next election — that is, how does he maximize

$$present\ value\ (PV) = \int_0^T We^{-rs}ds, \qquad (4\text{–}1)$$

subject to the constraint that $T = T(W)$, $(\partial T/\partial W) < 0$?[5] Or in words, how does he maximize the present value of this stream of wishes subject to the constraint that the higher the wish, the shorter the stream?

We can rewrite (4–1) as

$$PV = W\left[-\frac{1}{r}e^{-r \cdot T(W)} + \frac{1}{r}\right]. \qquad (4\text{–}2)$$

The first-order conditions for maximum present value with respect to W are thus

$$\frac{\partial PV}{\partial W} = e^{-r \cdot T(W)}\left(W\frac{\partial T}{\partial W} - \frac{1}{r}\right) + \frac{1}{r} = 0. \qquad (4\text{–}3)$$

The result given by (4–3) merely states that the present value of the flow of services from the wish is maximized where W is chosen so that (4–3) holds. To solve for an optimum W, it is necessary to specify a functional form for $T(W)$.

An economically interesting case is

$$T(W) = \log\frac{a}{W}, \qquad (4\text{–}4)$$

where a is some shift parameter, the determinants of which we will discuss presently. Two general properties of this function are useful. First,

$$\frac{\partial T}{\partial W} = -\frac{1}{W} < 0. \tag{4-5}$$

Second, the higher W, the more slowly $T(W)$ declines, since $(\partial^2 T/\partial W^2) = (1/W^2) > 0$.

By inserting this functional form in (4–3), we can solve for the optimum W. Thus,

$$\hat{W} = e \log a - \frac{\log [1 - \log (1 + r)]}{\log(1 + r)}. \tag{4-6}$$

So the optimum wage to set under the terms of the problem facing the typical legislator is given by equation (4–6).[6] For illustration, we discuss two economic properties of this result.

First, as the discount rate increases, the optimum wage increases — that is, it can easily be shown that

$$\frac{\partial(\log \hat{W})}{\partial r} = \left[\frac{\log(1 + r) - (r/1 + r)}{r^2} \right] > 0. \tag{4-7}$$

As the terms of this pay problem make clear, the major influence on the durability of the wage payment is the prospect for reelection, which depends on factors such as closeness of party rivalry, age of the legislator, and so forth.

Second, the shift parameter, a, can be stated as a function of certain aspects of legislatures. In general, the change in the optimum W for a change in any of the arguments of a will have the same sign as the change in a for the change in any of its determinants; for example, as we argue below, the number of representatives (R) should affect the success of the legislative union in the predictable way — that is, a larger number of legislators will frustrate the success of the wage cartel. Thus, from equation (4–7) we expect that

$$\frac{\partial(\log \hat{W})}{\partial R} = \frac{1}{a} \frac{\partial a}{\partial R} < 0. \tag{4-8}$$

In our test of the model below, we employ this general interpretation of a to derive testable implications about aspects of legislatures that are likely to be important in the wage-setting process.

To recap somewhat, the economic analogue to the Wish Fairy problem is not hard to draw. We know that entry is not entirely barred in legislatures and that tenure extending beyond the present term is not guaranteed. This means that the present value of a seat will be inversely related to the wage rate after some point, because higher wages will attract new entrants and alienate voters, both of which conditions dampen reelection prospects and offset the effect of increasing the wage on the present value of seats. Incumbents must thus trade off union wage gains and other benefits from being in office against the extra costs associated with increased competition to retain seats. This is precisely the economic content of the Wish Fairy problem, where legislative-pay bills apply after the next election. There is thus a determinate upper bound on the monopoly wage in our problem.

As a result of monopoly power in this labor market, then, wages in states where legislators can set their own wage will be higher on average (W_M in Figure 4-1) relative to states where the wage is set in the constitution (W_C). The legislative union predictably will have a substantial impact on relative wages because the demand for legislator services will be quite inelastic, as we posited earlier. This condition follows from the rules of derived demand in two related senses. First, there is only one legislature per state, so there is not a nonunion sector from which to buy output. Second, there are in general poor substitutes for the services of legislators (e.g., laws).

Furthermore, two aspects of legislatures related to the wage-setting process can be treated within the interpretation of the shift parameter, a, in our model.

First, the size of the legislature is analogous to the size of a cartel. A larger number of legislators should thus influence the success of the wage cartel in a negative manner. This is our expectation, although we recognize, following Stigler, that the range of variation in legislative sizes is not large and that as a result we may not be able to detect empirically the effect of the number of legislators on the wage-setting process.

Second, since members of this union must stand for reelection, they are not guaranteed lifetime tenure as union members. The relationship between tenure and pay is twofold: Higher pay promotes entry, and incumbents pay themselves more. Where there is free competition in entry into legislatures, we expect that tenure will be lower at higher rates of pay. Where there are monopolistic restrictions on entry (e.g., gerrymandering by incumbents or by the judiciary), we expect that tenure will be longer at higher rates of pay. We argue that the latter case is more likely to predominate in state legislatures and that therefore $[\partial(\log \hat{W})/\partial T] = (1/a)(\partial a/\partial T) > 0$; in other words, we expect that tenure will be longer at higher rates of pay.[7]

The conceptual experiment in Figure 4-1 consists of converting a state where the legislative wage is set in the constitution to one where the wage is set by statute. We contend that the conditions of supply in this market are relatively homogeneous across states but that we can observe demand differences across states. We can thus estimate a locus of market-equilibrium points over states that can be interpreted as a Marshallian supply curve of labor, that is, the wage per man-year that is necessary to generate specific quantities of legislative services. This gives us an empirical means of testing the union metaphor and its implications with respect to the relative pay of legislators.

A TEST OF RELATIVE WAGE IMPLICATIONS

A test of the implications of our model regarding relative legislator wages in union and nonunion states is summarized in the following equation (4-9) and is explained below:

wage per man-year = f(man-years per biennium, pay method, date
of state constitution, turnover, no. of
representatives).   (4-9)

The dependent variable, wage per man-year, is the annual wage of a legislator. Annual pay is measured as the average of a two-year period to overcome problems of annual versus biennial sessions. Biennial legislators would thus receive in one year twice the amount of this wage.

As in the case of other labor markets, the marginal product of labor will play a decisive role in wage determination. The practical problem for empirical purposes is to define the marginal product of a legislator (a task that continues to elude GNP accountants). We chose the number of legislators times the duration of the legislative session, which is simply man-years per biennium. As a supply variable, this measure picks up the duration of service; for example, in those cases where one legislator worked twice as long as another at the same annual wage, his wage per man-year would be one-half that of his counterpart. In principle, this measure of legislative output regressed against a measure of pay is analogous to an aggregate supply curve of legislative services across states.[8]

A dummy variable for pay method provides a direct test of the unionization hypothesis since it measures the degree of union power on average. It is anticipated that the dummy variable will have a positive sign — that is, states where legislators can set their own wage should exhibit higher wages.[9]

The date of the state constitution is entered to check for the unionization effect in the following sense: The trend in more recent state constitutions is toward more effective cartelization of the political process. This variable may thus capture an effect on wages independently of the degree of union power. We expect newer constitutions to reflect higher wages, and since the date of the state constitution is entered as the year of adoption, we expect the sign on this variable to be positive.

Our measure of union tenure is turnover in state senates and houses. Turnover is defined as the number of new legislators in 1974 divided by the size of the chamber. The turnover variable poses a causation problem. Does pay drive turnover, or does turnover drive pay? Two possibilities are interesting in this regard. First, high pay may be the result of low turnover. This is a monopoly argument in which tenure is longer at higher rates of pay due to entry restraints erected by incumbent politicians. Second, high pay may result in high turnover. This is a competitive result where high pay induces entry into political competition and tenure falls as a consequence. Since we have not modeled the pay-tenure problem explicitly, we will let the data suggest which type of argument (if either) prevails in practice.

The size of the senate or house is entered to check for the effect of numbers on union success. We expect that larger legislatures will be more difficult to organize and discipline as a wage cartel.

Conventional multiple-regression procedures were used to estimate the model. We present the results of only the logarithmic specification of the model because it offers a slightly better fit than the linear form, and we can thus economize in the presentation of results. The coefficients in equation (4–9) are estimated from 1974 data on the variables across states in the United States.[10]

Fitting the model by ordinary least squares yields the prediction

Table 4–2. Log Compensation of Legislators, 1974

Independent Variables	House	Senate
Man-years per biennium	.65	.71
	(2.85)*	(3.38)*
Pay method	1.09	1.25
	(3.86)*	(4.58)*
Date of state constitution	11.56	12.93
	(2.60)*	(3.03)*
Turnover	−.60	−.41
	(−.20)	(−2.17)*
No. of representatives	(−.46)	−.61
	(−1.27)	(−1.43)
Intercept	−82.37	−92.97
	(−2.44)*	(−2.87)*
R^2	.53	.58
$F_{5,36}$	8.02*	9.75*

SOURCE: See note 10.
NOTE: * — significant at the 5 percent level.

equations for legislative compensation given in Table 4–2. The results in Table 4–2 can be interpreted as the wage necessary to fill the legislature for a given amount of output, that is, a quasi-supply curve of state legislators for the United States as a whole. There are two prediction equations, one for state houses of representatives and one for state senates.

The output variable, man-years per biennium, turns out to be a useful predictor of legislative wages. The elasticity of wages with respect to this measure of output is .71 in the senate equation and .65 in the house equation. This means that a 100 percent increase in output requires a 65 to 71 percent increase in pay and that this relationship is quite inelastic.

Direct evidence on union power can be found by examining the dummy variable for pay method. This variable appears at high levels of statistical significance, and in order to examine its impact more closely, we convert the results into dollar terms. This is done in the following manner. Using the estimated coefficients in Table 4–2 and the actual mean values of the other independent variables (calculated over all states), we let pay method take on the values zero for constitutional states and one for union states and observe the change in ln wage.[11] We convert this change to dollars by taking antilogarithms. This procedure yields an estimate of an average effect of pay procedure in dollar terms, holding constant the levels of the other independent variables across states.[12] For the house equation this procedure predicts a wage of $5,802 for constitutional states and $17,257 for pay-by-statute states. This represents a 197 percent increase in legal pay. The results for the senate equation are analogous. The predicted senate wage is $5,170 in constitutional states and $18,045 in union states. This represents a 249 percent increase in legal pay. As we expected, then, given the extreme degree of inelasticity of demand in this labor market, the legislative union is astonishingly powerful. Compare these results, for example, to Lewis's finding that unionization in the United States led, on average, to a 10 to 15 percent excess of union over nonunion wages (as a percent of nonunion wages) as of the late 1950s.[13]

The variable on the date of the state constitution has the expected sign and appears at high levels of statistical significance. Since we interpret this variable as more recent, implying greater cartelization, the effect on wages is probably strengthened by the fact that even in states where the legislative wage is set in the constitution, a new wage and other cartel measures (such as entry restrictions) can be suggested by the legislature when the constitution is changed.

The negative coefficients on turnover support the argument that tenure is longer at higher rates of pay (remember that lower turnover implies longer tenure), and the results are statistically strong in the senate equation. We have some evidence, then, that turnover measures the effects of monopolistic restrictions on entry.

We find the expected negative signs on the coefficients on the number of representatives at reasonable levels of statistical significance (at the 16 and 22 percent levels, respectively). Larger legislatures thus tentatively appear to frustrate the operations of the wage cartel.

The model explains over half of the variation in legislative pay for both senates and houses. Three additional aspects of our results should be noted.

First, the inclusion of a variable (size of majority) to measure the degree of competitiveness among parties in our estimating equations adds nothing to the analysis. Such a variable does not affect the other results and shows no statistical credibility in its own right. We take this as evidence that parties do not play a prominent role in determining legislative wages and also as additional evidence that the appropriate analogue to competition in politics is not party competition but competition among incumbents and potential entrants.

Second, governors must sign legislative-pay bills, and we expect that they will therefore be cut in on wage cartel gains. In Chapter 7 we discuss gubernatorial compensation in more detail.

Third, it is tempting to argue that these results on legislator pay may be due to the generalized inflation in the United States in recent years. In response to such a concern we can report that the results hold up quite well for other recent cross-sections taken from the *Book of the States*. In Table 4–3, for example, are reported the results of estimating the legislative pay model on 1971 data.[14] As the reader can easily verify, the results are almost identical to those reported in Table 4–2, and the intervening period between the two cross-sections was a period of nontrivial U.S. inflation. Indeed, on theoretical grounds the normal presumption would be that inflation should not impact dramatically on the legislative pay results. As in the case of any other price or wage in the economy, monopoly power in the legislative pay market can explain *high* but not *rising* wages.

Table 4–3. Log Compensation of Legislators, 1971

Independent Variables	House	Senate
Man-years per biennium	0.675	0.645
	(2.80)*	(2.72)*
Pay method	1.007	0.940
	(3.00)*	(2.74)*
Date of state constitution	13.250	14.469
	(2.57)*	(2.88)*
No. of representatives	−0.998	−0.190
	(−2.39)*	(−0.38)
Intercept	−93.667	−105.815
	(−2.38)*	(−2.79)*
R^2	0.39	0.39
$F_{4, 43}$	6.97*	6.85*

SOURCE: Council of State Governments, *Books of the States, 1972–1973* (Lexington, Ky.: Iron Works Pike, 1972), various pages.

NOTE: *—significant at the 5 percent level.

WAGE PAY AND MALFEASANCE

We find that the union metaphor is a useful means of analyzing and explaining legislative pay. Nonetheless, our discussion begs the question of why states differ in their method of setting legislative pay. We postpone until later (Chapter 8) a complete discussion of this problem, but we note here that recent theories of the control of politicians and other public (and private) employees who must be "trusted" suggest an answer.[15]

Becker and Stigler stress that the way to control individuals in positions of trust, such as legislators, "is to raise the salaries of enforcers above what they could get elsewhere, by an amount that is inversely related to the probability of detection, and directly related to the size of bribes and other benefits from malfeasance. A difference in salaries imposes a cost of dismissal equal to the present value of the difference between the future earnings stream in enforcement and other occupations. This cost can more than offset the gain from malfeasance."[16] Or, put somewhat differently, they argue that "trust calls for a salary premium not necessarily because better quality persons are thereby attracted, but because higher salaries impose a cost on violations of trust."[17] Our results will suggest (Chapter 5) that outside earning activities will be more important to politicians where legislative pay is lower, as in states where their pay is set in the constitution. In higher-pay states, individuals who will find it less in their self-interest to seek outside earnings (e.g., bribes) will be attracted to legislative service. In other words, politicians will be less corrupt if they are paid more, and voters may view legislative determination of pay as a method of controlling malfeasance among politicians.

SUMMARY

The purpose of this chapter was to analyze the process in which the legal pay of legislators is determined. This process takes two forms across states, one that allows legislators to set their own pay and one that sets their pay in the state constitution. A model was developed to stress the differences in these two methods of legislator wage determination, and its basic prediction of a very pronounced monopoly effect in legislator pay in pay-by-statute states came through strongly in an empirical test.

NOTES

1. The quotations appear respectively in the following sources: R. W. Maddox and R. F. Fuguay, *State and Local Government*, 2nd ed. (Princeton, N.J.: Nostrand, 1966), p. 135; J. A. Straayer, *American State and Local Government* (Columbus, Ohio: Merrill, 1973), p. 93; Council of State Governments, *Book of the States, 1968–1969* (Chicago: Council of State Governments, 1968), p. 45; Council of State Governments, *Book of the States, 1972–1973* (Lexington, Ky.: Iron Works Pike, 1972), p. 54; and Council of State Governments, *Book of the States, 1974–1975* (Lexington, Ky.: Iron Works Pike, 1974), p. 59.

2. George J. Stigler, "The Sizes of Legislatures," *Journal of Legal Studies* 5 (January 1976):17.

3. There is also some use of pay commissions among states. These commissions are appointed by the legislature, and no elaborate theory of regulation is needed to explain why we treat these states as cases in which the legislature sets the wage.

4. For analytical simplicity, we rule out political comebacks.

5. For mathematical simplicity, we employ the continuous form of the present value function as an approximation to the discrete case.

6. This result holds for $r > 0$ — that is, when the discount rate is positive — and for $a > e$ and $a > W$.

7. In this respect, we follow the empirical results on turnover uncovered by W. Mark Crain ("On the Structure and Stability of Political Markets," *Journal of Political Economy* 85 [August 1977]: 829–42).

8. As a practical matter, however, other available proxies for the marginal product of a legislator (e.g., bills introduced) are highly correlated with man-years per biennium, and our results are not sensitive to the use of this particular definition.

9. Since it is relatively more costly to change the constitution than to pass normal legislation, a change in any exogenous factor dictating a change in the legislative wage would be more likely to be realized in a pay-by-statute state.

10. Data are from Council of State Governments, *Book of the States, 1976–1977* (Lexington, Ky.: Iron Works Pike, 1976), various pages. Due to the lack of data on one or more variables for 1974, Kansas, Louisiana, Minnesota, Mississippi, Nebraska, New Hampshire, South Carolina, and Virginia are omitted from this test. We are thus analyzing forty-two state legislatures.

11. This is equivalent in logarithms to letting pay method take on the values of 1 and e (i.e., ln pay method = 0 and 1) and observing the change in ln wage.

12. We chose to estimate the dollar results in this manner in order to present the "average" effect of unionization in this labor market. This obviously is not the only way to estimate the effect of unionization. It all depends on what

is held in the pound of ceteris paribus in terms of the mean values of the other independent variables; for example, we could use values for only constitutional states and predict the effect of unionization of a "typical" constitutional state, or we could use values for a single constitutional state and estimate the effect of unionizing that particular state. See Table 7-2 where we estimate the unionization effect for each individual state.

13. H. Gregg Lewis, *Unionism and Relative Wages in the United States* (Chicago: University of Chicago Press, 1963). For further evidence, consider the recent experience in Delaware. In 1972 the salary of Delaware legislators was constitutionally set at $6,000 per year. By late 1975 Delaware had converted to pay by statute, and legislator pay had been raised to $9,000 per year.

14. Turnover data were not available for the 1971 cross section, and Minnesota and Nebraska are excluded from the estimations because of lack of data on one or more variables for 1971.

15. Robert T. Barro, "The Control of Politicians: An Economic Model," *Public Choice* 14 (Spring 1973):19–42; and Gary S. Becker and George J. Stigler, "Law Enforcement, Malfeasance, and Compensation of Enforcers," *Journal of Legal Studies* 3 (January 1974):1–18.

16. Becker and Stigler, "Law Enforcement, Malfeasance, and Compensation of Enforcers," p. 6.

17. Ibid., p. 12.

5 THE OUTSIDE EARNINGS OF POLITICIANS

In this chapter we develop and test a theory of the labor supply of politicians from various occupational backgrounds. In our analysis, as in conventional theories of labor supply, individuals with the lowest reservation wage will be the first to be hired, or as it is more commonly called in this market — elected. If we can isolate those individuals and the characteristics of their opportunity costs that make their reservation wages low, we can identify what types of people will supply political labor at various wage levels. Moreover, to the extent that reservation wages are similar across occupational backgrounds, a standard labor supply–occupational choice model will provide an economic theory of the occupational composition of legislatures.

For a number of reasons we expect that the occupational background of legislators will cause their opportunity cost or reservation wage for legislative service to vary and therefore will cause different types of occupations to be disproportionately represented among legislators. There is one set of individuals that can efficiently combine legislative service with their primary employments to earn outside income as politicians. Lawyers predominate among these individuals because even though they may have high opportunity costs for serving, they also have a unique ability to internalize the outside returns from passing laws. Their reservation wage is thus below that of many other potential politicians. Rent-seeking agents in the polity can influence the lawyer-legislator because legal avenues to compensate lawyers exist that are not cheaply available to other occupations;[1] for example, it is quite legitimate for an electric utility to hire lawyer-legislators to perform ordinary legal business, such as property transfers, and pay them in excess of their marginal products with the implicit goal in mind of influencing a rate hearing. Though this type of payment arrangement might be technically illegal, the way that the payment is made and the legal shroud provided by the tradition of attorney-client privilege make it costly for voters and legal authorities to discern a conflict of interest involved in the arrangement. Such overpayments are not only more highly visible but are also more easily prosecuted in the case of nonlawyer-legislators. Firms could, for example, hire electrician-legislators at wages above their marginal products, but it seems clear that voters and legal authorities will more easily perceive this conflict of interest than the one posed by the case of the lawyer qua legislator.

The other side of the dichotomy of the occupations that are heavily represented among legislators is comprised of individuals who may be expected to face low opportunity costs for legislative service but who cannot efficiently combine legislative service with their primary employments to earn outside income as politicians. Farmers are the prototype of this legislator. Although the time spent legislating may be expensive for farmers during certain periods of the year, legislative sessions are often held between growing seasons when the timing of legislative work is not crucial to farmers. This is not the case, for example, with service workers and perhaps, among other reasons, explains the relative absence of these "low" opportunity-cost individuals among the ranks of legislators. Moreover, farmer-legislators are similar to the electrician-legislator discussed above. There is nothing to prevent attempts to purchase the services of farmer-legislators at prices above the prevailing market price for their services, but such attempts could be easily spotted by voters and legal authorities. Attempts to pay farmers prices above marginal cost are more cheaply detected because the marginal product of a farmer is readily measured. A hundred bushels of wheat command a specified market price, whereas the quality dimension of legal services makes quantity comparisons more costly.

It should also be stressed that as compared with the lawyer-legislator, the farmer-legislator will confront a smaller range of outside earning possibilities. Because of his legal training, each law applies to a lawyer in the sense that he has a comparative advantage at writing and interpreting its content. The class of possibilities in this regard is narrower for other occupations in the legislature. Lawyer-legislators will thus dominate the other occupations because they can internalize the *direct* returns from the class of all laws.

We will argue that there are basically two testable implications of this theory of the market for legislators. First, the market for legislators will clear by attracting more high-outside-earnings individuals (e.g., lawyers, business professionals, insurance representatives, and real estate executives) where legislator pay is low. Second, where legislator pay is high, we expect that individuals with higher reservation wages will be successful at supplying political labor (e.g., farmers, educators, and housewives). As we explain further below, we reject the alternative hypothesis that individuals are elected to legislatures because they are the members of a general class of individuals, such as a special-interest group.

The chapter proceeds as follows. Initially, we develop a theory of the supply of legislators from various occupational backgrounds. We then examine the explanatory power of the theory using data on the occupational composition of state legislatures in the United States. Finally, we offer some concluding remarks on the incentives of lawyer-legislators to keep legislator pay low in order to bar the entry of other occupations into legislative service.

THE MARKET FOR LEGISLATORS

The range of variation in the occupational composition of state legislatures is given for the entire United States in 1975 in Table 5–1. Lawyers and business professionals comprise 63 percent of all state legislators, farmers and homemakers make up 12 percent of the total, and a hodgepodge of other occupations, dominated by educators, constitute the remaining 25 percent. The task of our theory will be to

Table 5–1.   Occupations of State Legislators, 1975

Occupational Category	No. of Legislators	% of Total
Lawyer	1,681	22
Other professionals	428	6
Insurance	402	5
Entrepreneur/self-employed	1,195	16
Business executive/managerial	408	5
Real estate/construction	392	5
Agriculture	718	9
Communications/arts	204	3
Other business occupations	331	4
Education	602	8
Government employees	259	3
Nonprofit organizations	41	1
Labor union	44	1
Homemaker/student	201	3
Information not furnished	658	9

SOURCE: Insurance Information Institute, *Occupational Profile of State Legislators* (New York: Insurance Information Institute, 1976).

explain this variation in the occupational composition of state legislatures.

The returns from legislating are appropriable and consist of the wage pay (including perquisites) and outside earnings of politicians. The former returns come at taxpayer expense and accrue to all legislators. The latter returns derive from rent-seeking expenditures by special interests and take a variety of forms, such as bribes, business for a legislator's law firm, business for firms in which the legislator has a financial interest, postlegislative employment by special interests, and so on.[2]

As we have already stressed, there is a dichotomy in the types of occupations that can be efficiently combined with legislative service. There are persons whose opportunity costs for legislative service are low because they have a high outside earning potential while in office (lawyers). On the other hand, there are persons with relatively higher opportunity costs for legislative service on a part-time basis because they have less outside earning potential as legislators (farmers).[3] Because of their outside earning possibilities, lawyers are the first to commit themselves to political labor supply as the auctioneer calls out low wages. As the wage rate is increased, business professionals are the next occupational group to commit themselves because of their relative outside earning potential. Farmers and housewives respond next because even though they do not have high outside earning potential, their time costs are low since they do not have to forsake their primary employments completely when supplying political services.

The alternative hypothesis that special interests will try to elect a majority of their members to the legislature will not hold water. Consider the example of lawyers. While lawyers as an occupational class will benefit from the passage of many laws, all lawyers are free riders in this context. Lawyers may seek legislation as an interest group (ABA), but on this basis there is no reason to expect more lawyers in the legislature than members of any other interest group. Special interests apparently find it more efficient to organize and lobby for their rents than to try to elect a majority of their members to the legislature.[4] In Table 5–1, for example, although labor unions receive numerous benefits from state governments, union officials or representatives constitute only 1 percent of all state legislators.

Lawyers predominate in legislatures because even if they must forgo large fees while in legislative service, they can obtain earnings while serving to a degree that other occupations cannot. Lawyer-legislators can pass laws that primarily benefit themselves and that do not benefit lawyers as a class; for example, while any lawyer may represent clients before the state parole board, there may be a high correlation between having a lawyer who is also a state legislator and favorable decisions by the board. A law that requires a lawyer to handle appeals to the parole board appears on the surface to benefit all lawyers, yet the returns from such practice may be effectively limited to lawyer-legislators. The person who seeks a parole will generally have a more inelastic demand for the services of lawyer-legislators than for ordinary lawyers under these circumstances. What this means, of course, is that many such laws are just wealth transfers; hence, lawyer-legislators can receive a brokerage fee for services rendered.

The ability of the lawyer-legislators to internalize returns in this way is a function of the power of the legislature over the regulatory board. The legislature appoints the board, sets pay and expense allowances for members, and monitors board activities. In addition, we note that regulatory commissioners tend to be predominately either lawyers or business executives.[5] This is explicable by the fact that legislators will appoint members of their own class to these positions in order to reduce the information costs of finding out who will play the game according to the outside earning rules; for example, in South Carolina where circuit court judges are elected by the legislature, there has never been a judge elected who was not a legislator.[6]

Business professionals are attracted to legislative service for the same reasons that lawyers are — that is, they have both high opportunity costs for legislative service and high-outside-earning potential as legislators. Construction and real estate firms are thus in a better position to capture state contracts with direct representation of their firms in the legislature. Insurance firms seeking regulatory gains will have a more inelastic demand for the consulting services of the insuranceman-legislator than for insurance specialists in general. Overall, we expect the reservation wage of business professionals to be below that for farmers but above that of lawyers, because they are able to combine legislative service with outside earnings to a lesser extent than lawyers. This follows because the outside earning capabilities of the business professional intersect with a smaller amount of legislative activity, and this implication of our argument is borne out at a preliminary level in the percentages of these occupations listed in Table 5–1 relative to that listed for lawyers.

More specific examples of the role of lawyers and businessmen as legislators abound across states. Consider the insurance industry in Illinois.[7] Insurance members have been the largest occupational group in the Illinois legislature (next to lawyers) for years, and insuranceman-legislators have traditionally dominated the insurance committees in the Illinois General Assembly. Yet, as Orren stresses:

> To limit the insurance group to those members who list insurance as their official occupation is to greatly underestimate its natural strength. . . . Another source of support for the insurance industry is among the lawyers, many of whom count insurance companies as important clients.[8]

So while insuranceman-legislators are limited to a specific area of legislation in seeking outside returns, clients can retain lawyer-legislators across the whole spectrum of legislative activity. Lawyers are thus in a position to internalize returns across a broader range of legislation than legislators from other professional backgrounds. Other things the same, then, lawyers will have a lower reservation wage than businessmen for political service.

In sum, lawyer-legislators will face a larger range of outside earning possibilities than other occupations in the legislature. In some sense each law applies to a lawyer. The possibilities in this regard are much narrower for business professionals, entrepreneurs, and other professionals in the legislature.[9] The lawyer-legislator may represent clients before any regulatory board while other professionals have a more limited range of possibilities in this regard.[10]

We can operationalize this part of the analysis readily. Where legislator pay is low, the market for legislators will clear by attracting individuals, such as lawyers and business professionals, for whom legislative service can be efficiently combined with outside earnings. This implies that there should be *larger* proportions of lawyers and business professionals where legislator pay is *lower,* for then outside earnings are a larger fraction of total pay and legislators from these occupations have the lowest supply prices for political service. Lawyer-legislators dominate in this process because they can internalize the outside returns from legislative service more efficiently than their counterparts in other professions; in other words, legal means exist for rent seekers to compensate lawyer-legislators for services rendered to a much greater extent than other occupational classes of legislators.

The other side of the dichotomy of the occupations that are attracted into legislative service consists of individuals with low opportunity costs for serving, as well as a low ability to capture outside returns as legislators. These individuals consist primarily of farmers (see Table 5–1). We argue that farmers are attracted in disproportionate numbers to the legislature because they have a low opportunity cost for serving on a part-time basis during certain seasons of the year. Another example of such a legislator is homemakers who supply political labor because they generally have low opportunity costs for serving.

This part of our theory can also be easily operationalized. As the legislative wage is increased, we expect farmers, homemakers, and other low-opportunity-cost–low-outside-earning categories to respond positively to the legislator wage and win seats away from lawyers and businessmen.

It should be emphasized that these hypotheses are a statement about what will happen at the relevant behavioral margins. As legislator pay goes up, a larger number of farmers and housewives will seek office, a situation that will reduce the probability that lawyers will win seats. The expected returns to lawyer-legislators will thus fall at the margin since they must now spend more to capture or retain seats. The returns to all legislators will be equalized at the margin in electoral competition, and we expect that as legislator pay rises, more farmers and housewives will appear in legislatures as a result.

EMPIRICAL EVIDENCE FROM STATE LEGISLATURES

Our theory stresses that there is a continuous spectrum of individuals who can earn different degrees of outside income as legislators. At one end of the spectrum are high-opportunity-cost–high-outside-earning individuals, such as lawyers, and at the other end are low-opportunity-cost–low-outside-earning individuals, such as farmers. We break this spectrum of occupations into three sections in order to test our theory. The first section (model 1) offers an explanation of the percentage of lawyers across state legislatures. The second section (model 2) seeks to explain the percentage of state legislators from the categories in Table 5–1 of insurance, entrepreneurs/self-employed, business executive/managerial, real estate/construction, and education. We lump all these categories into one section in order to represent a class of high-opportunity-cost individuals who can efficiently combine legislative service with outside earnings, though not to the degree that lawyers can. The third section (model 3) offers an explanation of the percentage of legislators from the remaining categories in Table 5–1, which consist of low-opportunity-cost–low-outside-earning individuals, primarily from agricultural backgrounds.

Model 1

Equation (5–1) states model 1 as follows:

% lawyers in state legislatures $=$ f (1/legislator wage, average income of associate lawyers − legislator wage, voter turnout, % of lawyers in state population, associations with headquarters in a state). (5–1)

The percentage of lawyers across state legislatures is the dependent variable. Legislator wage is the legal pay received by a legislator, and we state a nonlinear model with respect to this variable by entering its reciprocal. Legislator wage provides a direct test of the outside earning hypothesis in that as legislator pay goes up, we expect the percentage of lawyer-legislators to fall. We thus expect a positive sign on the reciprocal of legislator wage. We estimate a nonlinear specification of legislator wage because of a composition effect in the supply of lawyer-legislators. As we stress in our theory, lawyers who are willing to concentrate on earning outside commissions will be drawn into legislative service by the level of base pay (legislative wage exclusive of outside earnings). The market-clearing function of outside commissions will thus peter out at some high level of base pay, and the excess demand for lawyer-legislators will then be accommodated solely by the legislator wage. Fitting legislator wage as a rectangular hyperbola captures the essence of such an effect in the market for lawyer-legislators. This specification is not crucial so long as we adjust for the proportion of lawyers in the state. The variable reflecting the difference between the average income of a young lawyer in a state and the legislative wage is a measure of the opportunity cost of a lawyer-legislator. We predict a negative sign here because as the opportunity cost of legislating rises, fewer lawyers who are capable of or willing to procure outside earnings will run for office — that is, as the value of the lawyer's marginal product at lawyering goes up, he or she will allocate more time to lawyering and less time to legislating and procuring legislative influence. As we argued earlier, the outside earning activities of legislators are linked to the passage of special-interest legislation to which voter-consumers will generally be opposed on the grounds that they will face higher prices or be deprived of wealth as a result. Voter turnout is our proxy for this effect, and we expect a negative sign on this variable because greater awareness of the outside activities of lawyer-legislators will lead to less likelihood that they will be elected. We enter the percentage of lawyers in the state population as a control variable; we expect more lawyers to be elected where there are more to run for office. The number of trade associations with headquarters in a state is our proxy for the outside earning potential of lawyer-legislators. Since we posit that it is primarily lawyers who can efficiently combine legislative service with outside earnings, we expect that the percentage of lawyers in legislatures will rise as the number of associations goes up — that is, where there are many outside earning possibilities, lawyers will find it more attractive to seek office. It is thus a direct implication of our model that as the number of trade associations goes up, the percentage of lawyer-legislators should also rise.[11]

We estimate equation (5–1) on a cross-section of data for 1974 on state legislatures in the United States.[12] Fitting the model by ordinary least squares yields the results in Table 5–2.[13] Specifications of this

Table 5-2. Model 1: Percentage of Lawyers in State Legislatures, 1975

Independent Variables	OLS Estimates
1/Legislator wage	4575.8
	(1.87)*
Average income of associate lawyers − legislator wage	−0.00034
	(−1.72)*
Voter turnout	−0.78
	(−7.03)*
% lawyers in state population	80.881
	(2.20)*
Associations with headquarters in a state	0.0037
	(1.17)
Constant term	44.67
	(7.74)*
R^2	.67
$F_{5,\,41}$	16.66*

SOURCE: Calculated from U.S. Bureau of the Census, *Census of Selected Service Industries, 1972*, Subject Series Legal Services, SC 72-5-4 (Washington, D.C.: Government Printing Office, 1975); Council of State Governments, *Book of the States, 1976–1977* (Lexington, Ky.: Iron Works Pike, 1976); Insurance Information Institute, *Occupational Profile*; U.S. Bureau of the Census, *Statistical Abstract of the United States, 1975* (Washington, D.C.: Government Printing Office, 1976); Gale Research Company, *Encyclopedia of Associations* (Detroit: Ruffner, 1973).

NOTE: * — significant at the 5 percent level.

equation including per capita state income or the length of the legislative session (or both) do not alter the results, and neither variable is significant in its own right.

All of the independent variables appear in the expected direction and at reasonable levels of statistical significance. We find the expected positive sign on the reciprocal of the legislator wage at a 5 percent level of significance. Voter turnout and the lawyers' opportunity cost variable carry the predicted negative signs and are significant at the 1 and 5 percent levels, respectively. The percentage of lawyers in the state population is positively related to the proportion of lawyer-legislators, as expected, at the 5 percent level of significance. The associations variable, which proxies outside earning possibilities, has the predicted positive sign at the somewhat more tentative level of statistical significance of 15 percent. This variable might also be a proxy for state size. We thus estimated model 1 without *ASSOC* and also with state population in lieu of *ASSOC*. The results of these estimations do not differ materially from those reported in Table 5–2. Overall, model 1 is able to explain 67 percent of the variation in the presence of lawyers in the state legislatures in our sample.

Careful inspection of equation (5–1) reveals that legislative pay is entered twice, once in reciprocal form and again when the opportunity cost of legislative service is specified. If we take the partial derivative of the percentage of lawyers with respect to legislator pay, holding opportunity cost constant, we find that the two are negatively related for all values of pay. This procedure allows us to measure the pure substitution supply response of lawyers to a change in the legislative wage. If the reader is concerned that the proper method of determining this response is to take the derivative and allow the wage component of opportunity cost to change, we can report that the estimation of equation (5–1), where legislator pay is not included in the opportunity cost measure, yields nearly the same results as reported in Table 5–2. In this slightly altered specification (model 1) the coefficient on legislator pay is everywhere negative, though at a slightly lower level of significance. The other coefficients are basically unchanged as are their levels of significance. These results are given in Table 5–3.

Model 2

Equation (5–2) states model 2, which seeks to explain the percentage of business professionals, entrepreneurs, and educators across state legislatures, as follows:

$$\begin{matrix} \% \text{ insurance, entrepreneur/} \\ \text{self-employed, business} \\ \text{executive/managerial, real} \\ \text{estate/construction, education} \end{matrix} = \begin{matrix} f(\text{legislator wage, voter} \\ \text{turnout, per capita state} \\ \text{expenditures}). \end{matrix} \quad (5\text{–}2)$$

As with lawyers, we expect the market for legislators to clear by attracting more members of these occupations where legislator pay is low. Legislator wage again provides a direct test of the outside earnings hypothesis. We enter a linear specification of this variable in model 2, and we consequently expect a negative sign in this case. We employ a linear specification because it offers a slightly better fit to the data. We obtain all the predicted signs at acceptable levels of

Table 5–3. Model 1': Percentage of Lawyers in State Legislatures, 1975

Independent Variables	OLS Estimates
Legislator wage	3157.27
	(1.32)
Average income of associate lawyers	−0.00025
	(−1.04)
Voter turnout	−0.81
	(−7.21)*
% of lawyers in state population	8441.96
	(2.24)*
Associations with headquarters in a state	0.0064
	(2.26)*
Constant term	46.82
	(6.95)*
R^2	.66
$F_{5,41}$	15.61*

SOURCE: See Table 5–2.
NOTE: * — significant at the 5 percent level.

statistical significance with a nonlinear specification of legislator wage, such as that employed in model 1. We also omit a proxy for the opportunity cost facing these occupations for legislative service since there is not one available that will conveniently serve this purpose for the group as a whole. For the same reasons outlined in the discussion of model 1, we expect a negative sign on voter turnout. We drop the associations variable and use per capita state expenditures as a proxy for outside earnings in model 2. We do this both because it works empirically, while the associations variable does not, and because it seems more consistent with our theoretical argument that the outside earning opportunities of lawyers are broader than those of business professionals — that is, lawyers can pass laws that promote the demand for their personal services across the entire range of special interests in a state (hence, the associations variable), while businessmen depend more directly on the presence of state contracts and state business for outside returns (hence, the per capita state expenditures variable). The alternative specification involving associations does not alter the other coefficients or their levels of significance.

The results of estimating model 2 by ordinary least squares (OLS) appear in Table 5–4. All of the variables have the predicted signs. Legislator wage and per capita state expenditures are significant at the 1 percent level, and voter turnout is significant at the 12 percent level. Our theory thus again predicts consistently for a spectrum of high-opportunity-cost–high-outside-earning legislators, and the model generally explains their presence across state legislatures quite well.

Additional evidence in favor of our theory can be found by examining the point elasticities (evaluated at the means) of legislator wage and voter turnout in models 1 and 2. The wage elasticities in models 1 and 2 are −0.0203 and −0.19, and the turnout elasticities are −1.35 and −0.12, respectively. Business professionals thus exhibit a great deal more sensitivity to pay and a great deal less sensitivity to voter turnout than lawyers. Both these results square nicely with the earlier argument that lawyers are relatively more adept at earning outside

Table 5–4. Model 2: Percentage of Insurance, Entrepreneur/Self-Employed, Business Executive/ Managerial, Real Estate/Construction, and Education Categories in State Legislatures, 1975

Independent Variables	OLS Estimates
Legislator wage	−.00076
	(−4.72)*
Voter turnout	−.12
	(−1.21)
Per capita state expenditures	0.01198
	(3.16)*
Constant term	44.34
	(9.64)*
R^2	.37
$F_{3,\ 43}$	8.48*

SOURCE: Council of State Governments, *Book of the States, 1975–1976* (Lexington, Ky.: Iron Works Pike, 1976); Insurance Information Institute, *Occupational Profile*; U.S. Bureau of the Census, *Statistical Abstract of the United States, 1975.*

NOTE: * — significant at the 5 percent level.

income than businessmen. A lower elasticity with respect to pay indicates that lawyers are less sensitive to changes in explicit pay, as they should be if they can garner more income on the outside margin. A higher elasticity with respect to voter turnout suggests that the more extensive outside activities of lawyers dampen their reelection prospects relatively more than the reelection prospects of businessmen, who are predictably less active on the outside margin.[14]

Model 3

$$\% \text{ all other } = \begin{array}{l} f(\text{legislator wage, voter turnout, \% of state in-} \\ \text{come from agriculture, associations with head-} \\ \text{quarters in a state}). \end{array} \quad (5\text{-}3)$$

Our theory suggests that individuals in all other categories, primarily persons from agricultural backgrounds, are not capable of procuring outside returns as legislators and that at higher legislative wages we should find a larger proportion of individuals in other categories in the legislature. We thus expect three sign reversals in model 3. First, we expect the proportion of these categories to increase as the legislator wage increases. Second, since voter turnout monitors the outside activities of legislators and these individuals are not productive at such activities in our theory, we predict a positive sign on voter turnout. Third, the associations variable should be negatively related to the proportion of low-opportunity-cost–low-outside-earning categories in state legislatures — that is, as outside earning possibilities fall in our model, more and more nonlawyers will be capable of winning elections because electoral competition from lawyers recedes. Finally, the proportion of income from the agricultural sector reflects the fact that in our model a farmer will find it easier to get elected where there is a greater reliance on agriculture in a state. If people associated with agriculture vote for farmers, then the farmer-legislators' campaign expenditures, for a given probability of election, will fall in states where agriculture is a greater proportion of state income.

The results in Table 5–5 strongly verify our expectations about the high-reservation-wage–low-outside-earning occupations. All the independent variables carry the predicted signs at levels of statistical significance of 5 percent or better. We obtain the expected sign on the variable that reflects the amount of agriculture in a state, or the ease

Table 5–5.   Model 3: Percentage of All Other Occupational Categories in State Legislatures, 1975

Independent Variables	OLS Estimates
Legislator wage	0.00056
	(2.00)*
Voter turnout	0.629
	(4.13)*
Percentage of state income from agriculture	0.0031
	(2.97)*
Associations with headquarters in a state	−0.0069
	(−1.78)*
Constant term	4.39
	(0.67)
R^2	.51
$F_{4,\,42}$	10.80*

SOURCE: Council of State Governments, *Book of the States, 1975–1976*; Insurance Information Institute, *Occupational Profile*; U.S. Bureau of the Census, *Statistical Abstract of the United States, 1975*; Gale Research Company, *Encyclopedia of Associations*.

NOTE: * — significant at the 5 percent level.

with which farmers can get elected. Perhaps most impressively, the sign reversals on legislator wage, voter turnout, and the associations variable strongly support our argument that individuals from these occupations cannot efficiently combine legislative service with outside earnings. We are also able to explain over half the variation in these types of occupations across the state legislatures in our sample.

Additional Points

First, the occupational groupings in models 2 and 3 are a judgment call on our part, but one that does not alter the results in a significant manner. We obtain results quite similar to those reported for models 2 and 3 if we break out the various occupations and estimate the same basic model for each occupation separately. Our groupings allow us primarily to economize in the presentation of results.

Second, all of our models are reduced-form supply-and-demand equations. We ignore problems of simultaneous equations bias since we obtain reasonable results from the reduced-form equations.

Third, to this point we have ignored the role of legislative size in our analysis. We argued earlier, however, that legislative influence would predictably be a monotonically decreasing function of the size of the legislature because more legislators will dilute the influence of each (Chapter 3). For this reason we would expect legislative size to obtain a negative sign in models 1 and 2 and a positive sign in model 3. Results of estimating the three models, including legislative size variables and New Hampshire in the estimations, are given in Tables 5–6 through 5–8.

We find the expected results on the legislative size variables in models 1 and 3 for legislatures with more than 250 members. The puzzle in the results is why the predicted effects tend to show up only in very large legislatures. The probable explanation goes as follows.

Table 5–6. Model 1 with Legislative Size

Independent Variables	OLS Estimates
1/Legislator wage	2666.28
	(1.57)*
Average income of associate lawyers − legislator wage	−0.00029
	(−1.41)*
Voter turnout	−0.74
	(−6.46)**
% lawyers in state population	8797.31
	(2.39)**
Associations with headquarters in a state	0.0039
	(1.22)
Legislative size	0.18
	(2.20)**
Legislative size squared	−0.00056
	(−2.43)**
Constant term	29.02
	(2.92)**
R^2	.69
$F_{7,\,40}$	12.97**

SOURCE: See Table 5–2.
NOTE: * — significant at the 10 percent level; ** — significant at the 5 percent level.

Table 5–7. Model 2 with Legislative Size

Independent Variables	OLS Estimates
Legislator wage	−0.00068
	(−4.20)*
Voter turnout	−0.13
	(−1.19)
Per capita state expenditures	11.02
	(2.44)*
Legislative size	0.001
	(0.02)
Legislative size squared	−0.000061
	(−0.44)
Constant term	45.65
	(4.99)*
R^2	.37
$F_{5,\,42}$	4.96*

SOURCE: See Table 5–4.
NOTE: * — significant at the 5 percent level.

Table 5–8. Model 3 with Legislative Size

Independent Variables	OLS Estimates
Legislator wage	0.00053
	(1.89)*
Voter turnout	0.61
	(3.77)*
Percentage of state income from agriculture	3.36×10^{10}
	(3.16)*
Associations with headquarters in a state	−0.0074
	(−1.79)*
Legislative size	−0.10
	(−1.27)
Legislative size squared	0.00039
	(2.15)*
Constant term	11.16
	(0.94)
R^2	.56
$F_{6,\,41}$	8.66*

SOURCE: See Table 5–5.
NOTE: * — significant at the 5 percent level.

We know that larger legislatures appear in states with higher income. Thus, even though the influence of individual legislators is diluted in larger legislatures, we observe a positive relationship between the proportion of lawyers and size of the legislature over this range because greater outside income possibilities are related to higher state income. Exactly the reverse argument applies to the sign reversals that we observe in the legislative size variables in Model 3. Legislative size does not affect the observed proportions of the occupations covered in model 2 in any statistically reliable sense.

LOW WAGE PAY AS AN ENTRY BARRIER IN POLITICS

At low rates of legislator pay, lawyer-legislators will be competing for a fixed number of seats in elections with only other lawyers or with individuals with a low opportunity cost for serving. Due to the ability of lawyers to capture outside earnings, legislative seats will be worth more to lawyers, their reservation wages will be lower, and they will therefore outspend and defeat other individuals for these seats.[15] Raising legislative pay will raise the present value of seats to all current and prospective legislators, but the relative increase will be the greatest for those who receive the smallest extra income for legislating. Higher wage pay for legislators will thus elicit a hardier brand of competition for lawyer-legislators at the polls. Thus, even though lawyers who get elected will earn quasi-rents as wage rises, their probability of getting elected is lower. So, for legislators another implication of our approach is that lawyer-legislators (and other legislators who fit this prototype) have incentives to keep wage pay low as a means to deter the entry of new competition at the polls and increase the present value of their seats. As we argued in Chapter 4, higher wage pay may therefore be an effective means of controlling malfeasance among politicians. Higher wage pay not only increases the costs of malfeasance to legislators but it also attracts individuals into politics who have less ability to seek outside returns.

Just because malfeasance is less, however, does not necessarily mean that we have a better system of government. We know that outside earnings motivate and control lawyer-legislators at low rates of wage pay. We get our public goods (roads and schools) as a by-product of this wealth-transfer process. We can only conjecture about the nature of the motivation and control of politicians who are attracted to the legislature at higher rates of wage pay; for example, since these individuals are unwilling or unable to seek outside returns as legislators, their legislative activities may be subject to less monitoring by voters, and they may seek nonpecuniary income in the form of the satisfaction derived from voting for their personal conceptions of the public interest. Whether this form of self-interest or that typified by the lawyer-legislator responding to special-interest rent seekers results in a better public economy is an open question.

SUMMARY

This chapter extended the previous analysis of legislator pay by developing and testing a theory of the outside income of legislators. The theory stressed the ability of certain occupations to combine legislating with outside income opportunities and suggested that these occupations should predominate in legislatures where the legal pay of legislators is low. This expectation, as well as several other basic aspects of the theory, was borne out strongly in a series of empirical tests.

NOTES

1. George J. Stigler, "The Theory of Economic Regulation," *Bell Journal of Economics and Management Science* 2 (Spring 1971):13, makes a similar point. "Why are so many politicians lawyers? — because everyone employs lawyers, so the congressman's firm is a suitable avenue of compensation, whereas a physician would have to be given bribes rather than patronage." We develop and test our theory primarily with reference to state legislators, for whom legislating is generally a part-time occupation. However, for precisely the reason that Stigler notes above — that lawyer-legislators can maintain residual claims in their law firms while serving — one could explain why there are so many lawyers in the U.S. Congress where service constitutes basically a full-time occupation. Also, the possibility should be noted that the outside returns to lawyer-legislators in the federal Congress may swamp the returns from private legal practice.

2. This argument is consistent with the role of the legislator as a broker in the market for legislation in the interest-group theory of government. There is an obvious relationship between legislator pay and the presence of occupations in the legislature that can internalize these extra earnings — that is, we are interested primarily in the labor-supply aspect of legislating. The

companion question of the determinants of the demand for special-interest legislation was treated in Chapter 3.

3. It appears that there is no occupation that combines the best of both characteristics, that is, low opportunity cost and the potential for high outside earnings.

4. We developed an analysis related to this point in Chapter 3. All legislators will, of course, vote for measures that favor their occupations, and if such measures pass, they will reap their *pro rata* share of occupational rents. As we stress in the text, however, all members of an occupation are free riders in this context, and this does not seem to be the reason that disproportionate numbers of certain occupations are attracted to legislative service. Nonetheless, special interests whose members can combine legislative service efficiently with outside earnings may find it less expensive to procure protective measures. Moreover, under some circumstances firms or businessmen may want particular benefits from the legislature and will seek election in order to obtain them.

5. See George J. Stigler, ''The Process of Economic Regulation,'' in Stigler, *The Citizen and the State* (Chicago: University of Chicago Press, 1975), pp. 145–66.

6. *Greenville News,* March 12, 1978.

7. See K. Orren, *Corporate Power and Social Change: The Politics of the Life Insurance Industry* (Baltimore: Johns Hopkins University Press, 1974).

8. Ibid., p. 50.

9. In our subsequent analysis we will treat educators analogously to business professionals. Education is a highly regulated and subsidized industry at the state level, and service in the legislature will enhance the educator's consulting and outside earning opportunities mightily.

10. Since all legislators can profit from legislative action through financial affiliations with private firms, we see no basis for distinguishing among occupations in this respect.

11. It might also be true that there are many trade associations where there are many lawyers in the legislature. On either ground we expect a positive relationship.

12. Nebraska and Wyoming are omitted from our tests because of missing data on one or more variables. We also omit New Hampshire from our tests, a state that at first blush seems wildly inconsistent with our theory. In New Hampshire there are 424 legislators who are paid $200 per biennium for their services, and most of these legislators are farmers and housewives. Why should lawyers not dominate the New Hampshire legislature at this extraordinarily low rate of legislator pay? The answer is consistent with our theory. The New Hampshire legislature is so large that the market price of legislative influence for an individual legislator is probably zero (see Chapter 3). Without recourse to outside earnings, opportunity costs for legislative service will

dictate that high-opportunity-cost individuals, such as lawyers, will stick to lawyering, and low-opportunity-cost individuals, such as farmers and house-wives, will take over the legislature. See George J. Stigler, "The Sizes of Legislatures," *Journal of Legal Studies* 5 (January 1976):17–34, for other types of analytical and empirical problems posed by the New England state legislatures. In general, we make no regional distinctions in our analysis. We did not expect any such distinctions on theoretical grounds, and several at-tempts to find them in the data were unsuccessful and failed to mitigate the other results.

13. The fact that the residuals across equations for each state sum to zero presents an estimating problem. Ordinary least squares will generally not be efficient if the covariance between errors across equations is not zero. Seem-ingly unrelated regressions (three-stage least squares, or 3SLS) estimation of all three equations simultaneously is not possible because the residual vari-ance-covariance matrix is singular. For discussions of a similar problem in share estimation, see E. R. Brendt and D. O. Wood, "Technology, Prices, and the Derived Demand for Energy," *Review of Economics and Statistics* 57 (August 1975):259–68; and L. R. Christensen and W. H. Greene, "Econ-omies of Scale in U.S. Electric Power Generation," *Journal of Political Economy* 84 (August 1976):655–76. This problem can be resolved by dropping one equation, but in general the results are sensitive to the equation deleted. However, A. P. Barten, "Maximum Likelihood Estimators of a Complete System of Demand Equations," *European Economic Review* 1 (Fall 1964):7–73, has shown that in a system of simultaneous equations, where the left-hand side variables sum to a constant, any equation can be deleted, and the results are invariant to the deleted equation *if* you have maximum likelihood esti-mates. Following J. Kmenta and R. F. Gilbert, "Small Sample Properties of Alternative Estimators of Seemingly Unrelated Regressions," *Journal of the American Statistical Association* 63 (December 1968):1180–1200, we employed the iterative Zellner efficient technique (I3SLS) to achieve maximum likeli-hood estimates. In fact, although this more involved estimation procedure allows us to solve an econometric problem, our results did not differ from those obtained from OLS estimation of each model separately. We thus stick with the simpler approach and report only the OLS results for the reader's inspection here.

14. It is tempting to argue that there may be a greater supply of businessmen in states where legislator pay is low or, more importantly, that legislator pay is low in response to the relative abundance of businessmen. Since we appar-ently do not control for such a supply effect, the negative relation between the fraction of business professionals and the legislative wage could be due to their greater numbers in the state population. We agree that it is appropriate to control for this effect, but data costs are insurmountable. We are, however, heartened that the supply of business professionals or their fraction in the

state population is probably correlated with state per capita expenditures, a correlation that suggests that we actually have controlled for such an effect.

15. There is an alternative theory that also explains the observed occupational composition of legislatures — politics is a luxury consumption good. Lower wage groups like farmers cannot afford to enter low-paying, high-consumption-value legislative jobs, while higher wage groups like rich lawyers can. Along the same lines, the negative relationship between voter turnout and the fraction of lawyers in the legislature can be explained by the hypothesis that lawyers are elected because they know the law best, and the demand for legislators with such knowledge is highest where the citizenry is least politically active — the states with the lowest turnout. This is certainly a conceivable way to approach the problem of political labor supply, and one consistent with other analyses of political behavior in the economic approach to politics; for example, the act of voting has been extensively analyzed as a luxury consumption activity. We, however, do not put much stock in this approach. If we are to have a *general* economic theory of labor supply, it seems inconsistent to us to postulate a special provision for political labor supply. Moreover, on this issue we are inclined to agree with George J. Stigler ("Economic Competition and Political Competition," *Public Choice* 13 [Fall 1972]:104), who argues that "the investment motive is rich in empirical implications, and the consumption motive is less well-endowed, so we should see how far we can carry the former analysis before we add the latter."

6 THE SUPPLY OF MAJORITY LEADERSHIP

Political competition is normally analyzed in both the popular and scholarly presses in terms of the competition of individual candidates for seats in electoral districts and in terms of the competition of parties for majority control of the legislature. An equally interesting manifestation of political competition takes place within political parties when politicians of the same stripe compete with one another for positions of power and authority in the party. In some respects the latter type of competition is not well understood, or perhaps we should say that it has not been taken on as an independent problem for analysis in the economic approach to politics; for example, it was recently observed that

> an all-powerful legislator would have no checks from competition, so his actions are limited not only by reelection — which cannot be better than

This chapter has been reprinted from Robert E. McCormick and Robert D. Tollison, "Rent-Seeking Competition in Political Parties," *Public Choice* 34 (1979):5–14, by permission of *Public Choice*.

a periodic event — but also by the division of powers among groups with different terms, different constituencies, and different incentives.[1]

While there is nothing wrong with this statement taken in the general context of Stigler's remarks, we feel that this view of legislative power tends to mask the nature of the constraints that competition within parties for positions of legislative authority tends to place on legislators such as majority leaders.

In order to explore the nature of competition within political parties further, we develop an explanation of competition for positions of majority leadership in this chapter. Our theory is elaborated in the first section to follow, and it contains two important aspects: One is that the size of the majority measures the number of potential competitors for the rents inherent in the position of majority leader; the other is that the extra legislative work involved in being majority leader will call forth extra pay by the normal dictates of labor supply theory. We test our theory in the second section below by trying to explain the extra wage pay received by majority leaders in U.S. state legislatures. For the reader's reference the extra wage pay per year in 1974 for majority leaders in state senates and houses of representatives is given in Table 6–1.[2] We note that extra pay for majority leaders differs between senate and house in ten states and ranges from no extra pay in several states to $30,500 yearly in Pennsylvania.

COMPETITION FOR MAJORITY LEADERSHIP

An economic interpretation of the function of a majority leader in a legislative setting consists in the view that this individual is an economic agent who brokers deals between demanders and suppliers of legislation. The majority leader thus frequently represents the views of demanders of legislation before those of suppliers, and vice versa. Ostensibly, this activity reduces transaction costs in the market for legislation. In cases where this activity is delegated to committees and their leaders, the role of the majority leader becomes analogous to that of an overseer-manager. His function in this case is to make committee assignments, route bills through the legislative process, schedule votes, and so forth.

In one sense the majority leader is the voice of the majority party, which translates into legislative power, or, in economics terminology,

Table 6–1.   Extra Pay for a Majority Leadership, 1974

State	Senate Leader Pay ($)	House Leader Pay ($)	State	Senate Leader Pay ($)	House Leader Pay ($)
Arizona	0	0	South Carolina	1,575	4,075
California	0	0	Maine	1,925	1,925
Hawaii	0	0	Connecticut	2,000	2,000
Missouri	0	0	Vermont	0	2,400
Nebraska	0	0	Oregon	2,640	2,640
New Mexico	0	0	Florida	3,000	3,000
South Dakota	0	0	Indiana	3,000	3,000
Texas	0	0	Colorado	3,570	3,570
Utah	0	0	Iowa	4,000	4,000
Washington	0	0	Kansas	4,200	4,200
New Hamsphire	50	50	Oklahoma	4,200	4,200
Wyoming	63	63	North Carolina	1,250	4,550
Alabama	72	72	Maryland	5,000	5,000
Wisconsin	0	75	Michigan	5,000	5,000
Nevada	146	146	Virginia	5,050	5,050
Arkansas	0	150	Tennessee	6,000	6,000
North Dakota	0	220	New Jersey	6,667	6,667
Idaho	250	250	Mississippi	6,900	6,900
Kentucky	300	300	Ohio	7,500	7,500
Montana	300	300	Illinois	10,000	10,000
Rhode Island	0	335	Georgia	2,800	17,800
Alaska	500	500	New York	21,000	21,000
Minnesota	580	580	Massachusetts	22,204	22,204
West Virginia	1,150	1,150	Louisiana	25,000	25,000
Delaware	1,150	1,150	Pennsylvania	30,500	30,500

SOURCE: Council of State Governments, *Book of the States, 1975–1976* (Lexington, Ky.: Iron Works Pike, 1976), pp. 54–55.

NOTE: In cases where daily pay was provided, days in session were calculated on the basis of actual days in session in 1973–74.

into rents. These rents are traceable to the fact that the allocative scheme of the legislature is not based on bidding for such items as office space and travel funds, but rather on allowing the majority leader to give these items out to members of his party. There will thus be competition from within the party for the rents associated with positions of majority leadership. As a simple working hypothesis, which we will quickly modify below, the competitors for majority leadership will include all the legislators in the majority party, and following the normal economic expectation, this competition will imply *lower* wages and the dissipation of rents for party bosses.

Yet in another sense the work involved for the majority leader in providing brokering services between demanders and suppliers of legislation and in handing out rents within the party is going to be a monotonic transformation of the size of the party; for example, where there are more party members to keep track of, the work load of the majority leader will increase. On this basis we expect that by the normal canons of labor supply theory, *higher* pay will be required to call forth extra effort by the majority leader.

Therein lies a dichotomy: A larger majority implies both lower and higher pay for a majority leader, in the first case on the grounds of rent-seeking competition within the party and in the second case on the grounds of the extra work involved in managing legislative transactions in a larger group. Our purpose in this section is to resolve this apparent paradox by stating a testable theory of competition for positions of legislative influence.

We consider first the relationship between majority leader work load and the size of the majority. We postulate simply that the transaction costs (e.g., the difficulty of reaching a consensus among suppliers of legislation) facing the majority leader rise at an increasing rate with respect to majority size and that the extra pay necessary to induce individuals to supply the service of organizing the legislative market must also increase at an increasing rate. Figure 6–1 illustrates such an effect.

The relationship between the rents associated with the majority leader's job and the number of competitors within the party for such positions is somewhat more complex. First, we postulate that the rents to be competed for by prospective candidates for majority leader increase at a *decreasing* rate with respect to size of majority. Our reasoning here is straightforward. Larger majorities are more difficult (costly) to organize and discipline in the supply of legislation. Beyond some point, then, diminishing returns (rents) with respect to majority size will set in.[3] Second, we postulate that the number of relevant competitors for the post of majority leader will increase at an *increasing* rate. Our reasoning is again straightforward. In small groups the transaction costs of finding the most capable leader are lower, and there are fewer qualified candidates. In larger groups, these transaction

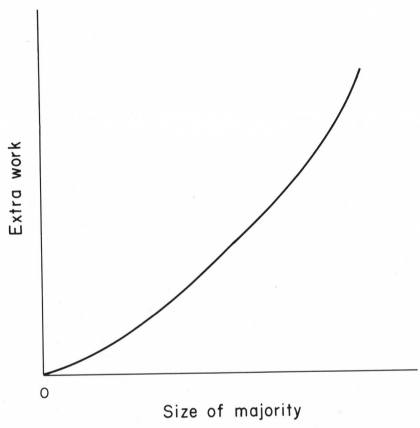

Figure 6–1. Extra Work Effect

costs are higher, inducing less capable candidates to compete for the majority leader position, and there also are more qualified candidates. For both reasons we expect the number of rent seekers to increase at an increasing rate with respect to group size. So the *net* effect on the rents inherent in being a majority leader, which we will proxy by the extra wage pay for such positions, will be dominated by the faster increase in the number of potential rent seekers within the party. Figure 6–2 illustrates this relation.

Putting the work aspects and the (net) rent-seeking aspects of the competition for majority leadership together in Figure 6–3, our theory

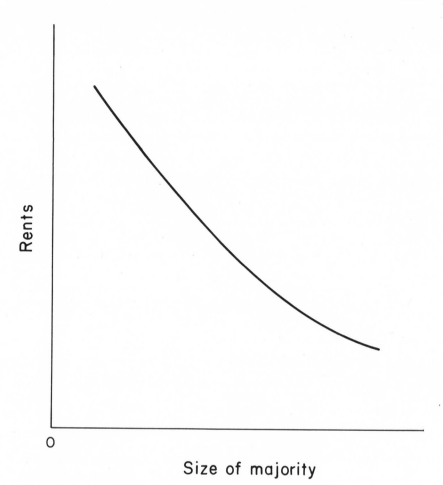

Figure 6–2. Rent Competition Effect

of majority leadership indicates that a u-shaped relationship will capture the combined effects of Figures 6–1 and 6–2. In region I we have
that the effect of increasing competition predominates, and extra pay
is lower as the size of the majority increases. In region II extra work
effort prevails.

    We will offer an empirical test of this theory of competition for
majority leadership in the next section. First, however, consider two
alternative hypotheses. In contrast to a competitive hypothesis, one

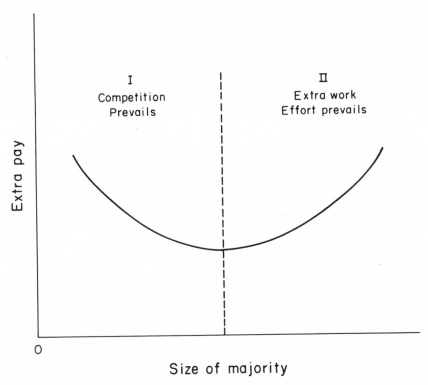

Figure 6–3. Extra Work and Rent Competition Effects Combined

could make a monopoly argument that the majority leader's power and therefore his extra pay (and implicitly his rents) are a *positive* function of the size of the majority. Given the presumption of diminishing rents beyond some majority size, the goal of the majority leader in this case would be to trade off the relations in our model among work load, rents, and majority size in such a way as to maximize the rental value of being majority leader. A second alternative hypothesis is simply that seniority uniquely determines who gets to be majority leader and that size of the majority should bear *no* relation to the extra pay and rents that go with these jobs. Perhaps time in office would be a relevant explanatory variable in this case. We now turn to an empirical test of our theory of majority leadership relative to these and potentially other alternative theories.

EMPIRICAL EVIDENCE FROM STATE LEGISLATURES

A test of our model of competition for party leadership is conveniently summarized by the following reduced-form equation:

$$\text{extra pay} = \frac{f(\text{bills introduced, number of representatives, size}}{\text{of majority, size of majority squared, turnover}).} \qquad (6\text{--}1)$$

The dependent variable, extra pay, is the additional yearly pay received by majority leaders above and beyond the normal pay of legislators (see Table 6–1), and we use this measure in equation (6–1) to proxy the extra rents associated with the job of majority leader.

Bills introduced and number of representatives are proxies for the work load of a majority leader. Bills introduced is self-explanatory; number of representatives (as distinct from size of majority below) is entered to account for the fact that the majority leader must also expend labor supply in dealing with the minority party. In the sense of our previous discussion, in brokering bills between the suppliers and demanders of legislation the transaction costs facing the majority leader are higher where bills introduced and number of representatives are larger; and by our argument that extra work load calls forth extra pay we expect positive signs on both these variables.

Size of majority is entered in equation (6–1) to proxy the number of competitors for the rents inherent in the majority leader position. By entering the square of majority size, we transform the data so that we can use OLS to estimate equation (6–1) and also to proxy first diminishing rents due to an increased number of competitors and then increasing pay due to larger work loads. We expect that the linear term will be negative with the influence of additional competitors predominating over an initial range of majority sizes, but we expect that beyond some point the squared term will start to dominate, indicating that the extra work load associated with larger majorities overwhelms the effect of extra competitors. Size of majority and its square thus capture the essence of our theoretical presuppositions as given in the discussion surrounding Figure 6–3. Turnover in the legislature is entered in equation (6–1) and is defined as the number of new legislators divided by the size of the chamber. Turnover has two distinct effects in our model. It can be seen basically as a shift parameter in Figure 6–1 — that is, holding size of the majority constant, lower turnover leads to less work effort and to a lower marginal product for the majority leader; for example, it is now easier to obtain a consensus of the suppliers of legislation to present to the demanders. Less work should evoke less pay on these grounds. Yet lower turnover also implies that the majority leader's function as a broker is more valuable to demanders and suppliers of legislation because there is now less uncertainty over the delivery of legislative deals. On these grounds, lower turnover leads to more rents associated with the majority leader position. The extra work and extra rent aspects of our model thereby lead to different implications about the expected sign on turnover in equation (6–1), and an empirical resolution of the actual sign is necessary.

We estimate equation (6–1) based upon a cross-section of state senates and houses of representatives for 1974.[4] The results of separate estimations for state senates and houses of representatives are given in Table 6–2.[5]

The results for the house equation strongly supprt our theoretical expectations. Bills introduced and number of representatives appear in the expected direction and at high levels of statistical significance.

Table 6–2. Extra Pay for Majority Leaders: Regression Results

Independent Variables	Senate	House
Bills introduced	0.86	0.46
	(4.59)*	(2.52)*
Number of representatives	245.10	150.90
	(1.97)*	(4.00)*
Size of majority	−211.92	−232.86
	(−0.45)	(−2.76)*
Size of majority squared	0.77	0.76
	(0.11)	(2.06)*
Turnover	−16,752.01	−1,459.68
	(−1.73)	(−0.27)
Intercept	2,353.61	−1,189.74
	(−0.41)	(−0.33)
R^2	.54	.62
$F_{5, 37}$	8.56*	
$F_{5, 40}$		13.24*
N	43	46

SOURCE: Calculated from Council of State Governments, *Book of the States, 1975–1976*, pp. 54–55.

NOTE: * — significant at the 5 percent level.

Extra labor supply by the majority leader calls forth extra pay. The sign pattern and significance levels on size of majority and its square also support our theoretical expectations. As the number of competitors for the job of majority leader increases, extra pay decreases at a decreasing rate. Using the estimated equation and minimizing extra pay with respect to size of the majority, we find that the effect of competition for rents predominates the work load effect in our model up to a majority size of approximately 319 members.[6] The negative sign on turnover is also consistent with the fact that the rent competition effect outweighs the work effect in our model; that is, lower turnover leads to higher extra pay. But both effects are so confounded in the data that we do not get a statistically significant result for this variable. We also note that we have a quite good general explanation ($R^2 = .62$) of pay differentials received by majority leaders across state houses of representatives.

The results for the senate equation are different from those for the house equation. Like the house equation, the extra work variables appear in the expected direction and at high levels of statistical significance. Unlike the house equation the number of competitors and work load arguments embodied in the size of majority variables does not stand up for state senates; yet neither does the alternative monopoly argument since we do not observe positive signs on these variables. We basically observe no relationship between extra pay and the size of majority variables in state senates. We interpret this evidence as indicating that seniority is the most likely explanation of who gets to be majority leader in state senates; that is, where promotion to majority leader is solely a function of years of service, one would expect to find coefficients on the size of the majority variables that are not significantly different from zero. Time in office would be the most important determinant of who became majority leader in this case.[7] Finally, turnover appears with a negative sign that is significant at the 10 percent level. The fact that lower turnover leads to higher pay again indicates that in terms of our model the rent competition effect outweighs the work effect with respect to the turnover variable in state senates.

Our results offer some preliminary support for an economic theory of competition within parties for positions of legislative leadership. This competition will dissipate the rents associated with the wage pay, perquisites, and outside earnings of these positions. As was the case with regular compensation, we expect that where the wage pay and perquisites for majority leaders are low, more individuals who can efficiently combine outside earnings with these positions will compete for and capture them. This explains why lawyers are the dominant occupational group not only among legislators in general but also among majority leaders in particular. Yet there are no "free" outside rents in this case. The competition we observe with respect to the extra wage pay and perquisites that go with these positions will also dissipate the rents associated with their outside earning possibilities. As outside earning possibilities rise, entry will be attracted, and incumbent majority leaders will have to expend resources to resist potential competition for their jobs.

SUMMARY

In this chapter a theory of competition for powerful positions in the legislature was formulated and tested. Size of the majority was the important variable in the theory in that it proxied both the extent of competition for leadership positions and the work load that the leadership must carry. The evidence indicates that of these two effects, the effect of competition for leadership positions within the majority is the more important one in determining the level of extra pay that majority leaders receive.

NOTES

1. George J. Stigler, "The Sizes of Legislatures," *Journal of Legal Studies* 5 (January 1976):19.
2. Extra expense allowances are found in only four cases — North Carolina, Pennsylvania, Tennessee, and Vermont. We include these allowances with extra pay for these states.
3. From some empirical evidence on this point, see W. Mark Crain and Robert D. Tollison, "Campaign Expenditures and Political Competition," *Journal of Law and Economics* 19 (April 1976):177–88.
4. Our data are taken from Council of State Governments, *Book of the States, 1975–1976* (Lexington, Ky.: Iron Works Pike, 1976). Several states are dropped from our tests because of the absence of data on one or more variables: Nebraska is omitted from both prediction equations; Kansas, Louisiana, Minnesota, Mississippi, South Carolina, and Virginia are dropped from the senate equation; and Louisiana, Mississippi, and New Hampshire are not

included in the house equation. We include states where majority leaders receive no extra pay because these observations are consistent with our theory — that is, competition for majority leadership can be sufficiently intense to drive extra wage pay to zero.

5. The implicit assumption of a bicameral approach to testing our theory empirically is that each house autonomously determines extra pay for its majority leader. It is true, however, that extra pay is the same in the senate and house of representatives in forty states, a fact that suggests some sort of interaction between the two chambers in determining extra pay for majority leaders that our bicameral approach to empirical testing does not capture. We can report, however, that estimating equation (6–1) on a combined sample of senates and houses, using simple averages of the right-hand side variables, yields all the expected signs at acceptable levels of statistical significance (except the coefficient on the turnover variable). A unicameral approach to testing our theory also explains about 70 percent of the variation in extra pay for majority leaders across states.

6. The lower house of the New Hampshire legislature, which has 400 members, is the only case among the American states in which it is even arithmetically possible to have a majority of 319 members. Since New Hampshire is excluded from our sample, the competitive effect of increasing the size of the majority dominates the work load effect entirely.

7. We also note that state senates are generally smaller than state houses of representatives and that therefore the transaction costs of finding an able leader are also generally lower in state senates. Thus, in our model increasing size of the majority over party sizes that are typically small may not produce the u-shaped effect that we predict. The nonresults on the majority variables in the senate equation may also be interpreted in this light.

7 THE DETERMINANTS OF EXECUTIVE BRANCH COMPENSATION

In the literature on the economic approach to politics and regulation the role of the executive branch of government has largely escaped the attention of scholars. Most analysis in this area, and in public choice generally, has focused on legislative behavior. Yet in our federal system of checks and balances, a tripartite system for legislation exists. To become a law, a measure must secure the approval of both houses of the legislature, the chief executive, and, if a subsequent dispute arises over the validity of the law, the judiciary. In a federal system the various branches of government are, in effect, constituted as separate legislative bodies. The chief executive, for example, through the use of the veto power, represents a third house of the legislature. Thus, in a practical, institutional sense the economic approach to analyzing politics is incomplete without some consideration of the behavior of the executive and judicial branches of government.[1]

Our theoretical approach to explaining governmental behavior is built around the concept of politicians as brokers of wealth transfers, as outlined in the discussion in Chapter 2. Recall that in that discussion, the brokers possessed the enforcement power to compel the transfers for which they were able to match demanders and suppliers. In practice this enforcement power is typically under the control of the executive branch, and we will therefore treat the chief executive as an enforcer of the wealth transfers negotiated by the legislature in our theory. Thus, the legislator plays the role of auctioneer, and the chief executive the role of enforcer in our approach. Why the two functions are separated (checks and balances), if indeed they can be viewed as separate (collusion), is an interesting question in its own right, but one we will not address here. We simply accept political institutions as they presently exist and seek in a very preliminary way to explore the role of the executive branch in the wealth-transfer process heretofore outlined in this book. Since our primary emphasis has been on the returns to political brokers in this process, our primary interest in this chapter will be in how the chief executive shares in these returns. As before, we will continue to use state governments as a cross-sectional basis for elaborating and testing our theory. Our main order of business in this chapter will thus be to present and test a model of gubernatorial compensation.

GUBERNATORIAL COMPENSATION

In a federal system of legislation the governor must sign legislative pay bills before they can become law. Thus, even where legislators can set their own pay, as analyzed in Chapter 4, the governor must still ratify such agreements before they can be implemented. Under these conditions the governor's signature will have a certain value to the legislature, and this value can be manifested in any number of ways; for example, it might take the form of the passage of pet gubernatorial legislation, acquiescence to gubernatorial appointments, or direct cash payments. Of course, the bargaining process between the governor and the legislature over such matters is a classic bilateral monopoly situation. Agreement implies that each party needs the other, but for the usual reasons we cannot exactly predict the distributional outcome of the bargaining. All we can say is that each party would be expected to share in the relevant gains of legislative and executive branch cooperation.

The governor's wage is a legal and conveniently observable avenue of compensation available to the legislature in this bargaining process.

And since it is conveniently observable, we will focus on gubernatorial compensation as a measurable consequence of the outcome of bilateral bargaining between the governor and the legislature. Thus, even though governors will surely extract some of their favors in kind, their wages are a convenient proxy for their portion of the benefits from wage cartelization.

If this argument about bilateral monopoly is correct, then gubernatorial pay not only will be determined by the size of the management problem facing the governor (the extent of state government activity), as has been argued elsewhere, but will also be directly related to the wage cartel gains in the legislature, as described in Chapter 4;[2] in other words, where the legislature can set its own pay and can *also* set the pay of the governor, the governor's pay, because his signature is essential to the wage cartelization process, will be related to the degree of legislative wage-setting power.

Gubernatorial compensation across the states in the United States is given in Table 7–1 for 1975. A practical, but important, fact about gubernatorial pay across states is that in only two states, Arkansas and Maryland, is the governor's wage set in the state constitution. The remaining forty-eight states allow the legislature to set the governor's pay, given certain provisos (e.g., that the governor's pay be neither raised nor lowered until he has stood for reelection).

Given this institutional background, we postulate the following model of how governors share in legislative wage cartel gains:

$$\log G = g_1 + g_2 \log (GPM) + g_3 \log (SB) + g_4 \log (YPC) + g_5 \log (Y) + g_6 \log (POP) + \mu,$$

where

G = gubernatorial pay as given in Table 7–1;
SB = total state government expenditures;
YPC = state personal income per capita;
Y = state personal income;
POP = state population;
μ = a random error term.

GPM is our measure of the governor's share of wage cartel gains, and its derivation requires a more detailed discussion. Where legislator pay is high because legislators set their own pay and where legislators can also set the pay of the governor, the governor's wage, G, will be

Table 7-1. Gubernatorial Compensation, 1975

State	Compensation ($)	State	Compensation ($)
Alabama	28,955	Montana	30,000
Alaska	50,000	Nebraska	25,000
Arizona	40,000	Nevada	40,000
Arkansas	10,000	New Hampshire	34,070
California	49,100	New Jersey	60,000
Colorado	40,000	New Mexico	35,000
Connecticut	42,000	New York	85,000
Delaware	35,000	North Carolina	38,500
Florida	50,000	North Dakota	18,000
Georgia	50,000	Ohio	50,000
Hawaii	46,000	Oklahoma	42,500
Idaho	33,000	Oregon	38,500
Illinois	50,000	Pennsylvania	60,000
Indiana	37,000	Rhode Island	42,500
Iowa	40,000	South Carolina	39,000
Kansas	35,000	South Dakota	27,500
Kentucky	35,000	Tennessee	50,000
Louisiana	50,000	Texas	65,000
Maine	35,000	Utah	35,000
Maryland	25,000	Vermont	36,100
Massachusetts	40,000	Virginia	50,000
Michigan	45,000	Washington	42,150
Minnesota	41,000	West Virginia	35,000
Mississippi	43,000	Wisconsin	44,292
Missouri	37,500	Wyoming	37,500

SOURCE: Council of State Governments, *Book of the States, 1975–1976* (Lexington, Ky.: Iron Works Pike, 1976).

higher by some fraction of the legislative wage cartelization effect. The greater the power of the legislative wage cartel, the bigger the governor's salary will be, other things being equal. *GPM* is designed to pick up this relationship. We obtain estimates of *GPM* by calculating for each state in our sample the legislative wage cartelization effects. These calculations are performed in the fashion suggested in Chapter 4 using the prediction equations in Table 4–3. These individual state estimates are reported in Table 7–2. *ETPW* is the expected state legislative wage if the legislators can set their own wage, and *ETPWO* is the expected wage if legislative pay is set in the state constitution.

Table 7-2. Estimates of Legislative Wage Cartel Effects, 1974

State	ETPW	ETPWO	GPM
Alabama	6096.41	1895.44	0
Alaska	12367.7	3845.25	8522.42
Arizona	13018.8	4047.69	8971.09
Arkansas	17262.2	5367.02	0
California	22465.5	6984.77	15480.7
Colorado	11380.9	3538.44	7842.43
Connecticut	17442.5	5423.06	12019.4
Delaware	9500.08	2953.68	6546.39
Florida	13931.2	4331.37	9599.85
Georgia	12096.5	3760.95	8335.57
Hawaii	13328.5	4143.98	9184.52
Idaho	9004.77	2799.69	0
Illinois	26207.3	8148.15	18059.2
Indiana	6873.46	2137.04	4736.42
Iowa	11814.7	3673.34	8141.39
Kentucky	9832.58	3057.06	6775.52
Maine	8494.01	2640.88	5853.12
Maryland	8681.41	2699.15	0
Massachusetts	10542.7	3277.85	7264.87
Michigan	25466.2	7917.75	17548.5
Missouri	25684.8	7985.70	17699.1
Montana	8327.58	2589.14	5738.44
Nevada	8153.39	2534.98	5618.41
New Jersey	12148.5	3777.11	8371.39
New Mexico	9055.29	2815.39	0
New York	14208.5	4417.57	9790.90
North Carolina	18935.1	5887.14	13048.0
North Dakota	10102.4	3140.97	0
Ohio	17324.7	5386.44	11938.2
Oklahoma	14098.8	4313.48	9715.35
Oregon	15323.1	4764.14	10559.0
Pennsylvania	14233.0	4425.20	9807.80
Rhode Island	7938.74	2468.25	0
South Dakota	7097.35	2206.65	4890.70
Tennessee	8246.83	2564.04	5682.80
Texas	15473.3	4810.84	0
Utah	7012.07	2180.13	0
Vermont	5365.48	1668.19	3697.29
Washington	10153.7	1668.19	3697.29
West Virginia	6806.54	3156.89	6996.77
Wisconsin	9786.40	2116.23	4690.31
Wyoming	4793.15	6743.70	3302.91

SOURCE: See note 3.

The resulting estimates of *GPM* are given in the last column of Table 7–2.[3] If legislators can set their own pay and can set G as well, then *GPM* is the difference between the expected legislative wage when legislators set their own pay (*ETPW*) and the expected legislative wage if set constitutionally (*ETPWO*). If either the legislative wage or G is set constitutionally, then *GPM* is set to zero. Essentially, then, our expectation is that gubernatorial pay will depend on the predicted level of legislative wage cartel gains across states and on whether the legislators can set the governor's pay. Where the latter condition holds, we expect that when the cartel gains are higher, the governor's share in them will be higher.

Several versions of the gubernatorial pay equation were estimated by ordinary least squares, and the results of the estimations are given in Table 7–3.[4] The results give very clear support to the hypothesis that the governor's signature is relatively more valuable where the wage cartel gains are higher. The *GPM* variable is positive and statistically significant in all specifications. However, the elasticity estimate of *GPM*, 0.03, suggests that governors are not the strong parties

Table 7–3. Log Compensation of Governors, 1974

Independent Variable	Coefficient/t-statistic			
Intercept	8.50 (1.96)*	6.15 (2.20)**	8.50 (1.96)*	3.86 (1.31)
GPM	0.027 (2.13)**	0.027 (2.15)**	0.027 (2.13)**	0.028 (2.19)**
SB	0.312 (1.44)*	0.161 (3.69)***	0.312 (1.44)*	
YPC	0.175 (0.43)	0.344 (1.05)	0.312 (0.934)	0.383 (1.14)
Y			−0.137 (−0.71)	0.134 (3.40)***
POP	−0.137 (0.71)			
R^2	0.45	0.44	0.45	0.41
F	7.43***	9.87***	7.43***	8.97***

SOURCE: See note 4.

NOTE: * — significant at the 10 percent level; ** — significant at the 5 percent level; *** — significant at the 1 percent level.

in these bilateral negotiations. They are, in effect, obtaining only a fraction of the pay increases resultant from cartelization. The other variables in the various specifications are essentially proxies for the management problem facing the governor. Thus, variables such as personal income, personal income per capita, and the size of state government have a predictably positive effect on gubernatorial compensation. These measures of the level of economic activity reflect the governor's work load in overseeing wealth redistributions; for example, he must manage the state bureaucracies, which in turn carry out the wealth-transfer mandates specified in legislation passed by the legislature and signed by the governor. Like his counterpart in private firms, therefore, the governor is compensated in relation to the size of his "firm."[5] Moreover, with a simple model we are able to explain almost half of the variation in gubernatorial pay across the states in our sample.

Finally, we should note that alternative specifications of our governor's pay equation do not materially affect the results given in Table 7-3; for example, governors' term lengths, succession rights, the number of gubernatorial appointments, and whether the governor's party and the legislative majority coincide make no substantive contribution to the model and do not affect the reported results.

THE QUESTION OF MALFEASANCE

Earlier, we discussed the Becker-Stigler theory of contractual malfeasance as it applied to the pay of state legislators. Then we briefly argued that higher pay was a means to control legislator malfeasance because to the individual legislator higher pay made malfeasance more costly in terms of losing one's seat. Further, in Chapter 5 we argued that higher legislator pay induced the entry into politics of individuals who do not have a comparative advantage at legislative malfeasance. Higher pay thus elicits a type of legislator who is more costly to compensate on the outside margin for arranging wealth transfers. These types of arguments suggest that higher pay for legislators is a means of channeling their behavior away, for example, from outside earnings. A similar argument obviously applies to governors and to the types of individuals (that is, their occupational backgrounds) who are attracted to run for governor. Lorderer has advanced such a pay and malfeasance argument for governors, though he does not present evidence on the occupational characteristics of governors.[6]

Such an approach to gubernatorial compensation and to political compensation in general is important and useful. Voters may wish to control malfeasance by politicians, and higher pay is one means of doing so (making them forfeit their pensions when caught in wrongdoing is another means). However, arguments of this sort, including the one we made earlier about state legislators, are plagued by problems of interpretation; for example, are the rules of the game, as embodied in state constitutions, written by the voters as a means to control malfeasance or are they written by interest groups to insure an efficient wealth-transfer process? Is the governor paid more to police governmental malfeasance or to expend greater efforts to carry out and police wealth-transfer contracts with interest groups? Are social contracts a means of controlling politicians or a means by which interest groups and politicians control us? Until we have a model that explains how the rules of the game are written and change over time, malfeasance arguments, such as that made by Lorderer and us, are difficult to evaluate. While we do not have any definitive answers to these questions, we do have some preliminary thoughts along these lines that we propose to offer the reader in our final chapter.

SUMMARY

Our model of political brokers was extended in this chapter to include the executive branch of government. The governor was treated as the enforcer of wealth transfers approved by the legislature, and this model was tested using data on gubernatorial pay. The results were supportive of the underlying theory in that gubernatorial pay was related to the predicted level of legislative wage cartel gains.

NOTES

1. We do not mean to imply that the record is completely devoid of analysis germane to executive and judicial behavior. In Chapter 1 we noted the pioneering study of William Landes and Richard Posner, "The Independent Judiciary in an Interest-Group Perspective," *Journal of Law and Economics* 18 (December 1975):875–901. Also, the economic theory of bureaucracy, as

given by Niskanen, surely pertains to important aspects of executive branch behavior; see William A. Niskanen, Jr., *Bureaucracy and Representative Government* (Chicago: Aldine-Atherton, 1971). Finally, for an attempt to point out the similarity between the nullification power of judges in the Landes-Posner theory and the veto power of the chief executive, see W. Mark Crain and Robert D. Tollison, "The Executive Branch in the Interest-Group Theory of Government," *Journal of Legal Studies* 8 (January 1979):165–75.

2. See W. Mark Crain and Robert D. Tollison, "State Budget Sizes and the Marginal Productivity of Governors," *Public Choice* 27 (Fall 1976):91–96.

3. We estimated the individual state cartelization effects for legislators by using a joint legislative wage equation rather than a separate house and senate equation. Our procedure for calculating *GPM* is given as follows:

$$GPM = PMG \cdot PM \cdot (ETPW - ETPWO),$$

where

PMG = 0 for states where gubernatorial compensation is constitutionally established (Maryland and Arkansas), and 1 otherwise;

PM = 0 for states where legislative wage is constitutionally established, and 1 otherwise;

$ETPWO = \exp[-87.1 + 0.63 \ln(Q_L) + 12.1 \ln(DSC) - 0.32 \ln(TURN) - 0.47 \ln(SIZE) + .227]$,

where

Q_L = quantity supplied of legislative services (size of legislature × length of legislative session);

$SIZE$ = number of senators plus number of representatives;

DSC = date of enactment of the present state constitution;

$TURN$ = proportion of new members in the legislature;

$ETPW = EPWO + \exp[1.168]$.

4. The data for the estimations in Table 7–3 come from Council of State Governments, *Book of the States, 1975–1976* (Lexington, Ky.: Iron Works Pike, 1976); and *Statistical Abstract of the United States, 1976* (Washington, D.C.: Government Printing Office). As before, several states are not included because of missing data. These include Kansas, Louisiana, Minnesota, Mississippi, Nebraska, New Hampshire, South Carolina, and Virginia.

5. See Armen A. Alchian and William R. Allen, *University Economics,* 3rd ed. (Belmont, Calif.: Wadsworth, 1972), pp. 425, 827, for this argument about managerial pay in private firms.

6. See Claudio Lorderer, "The Monitored Governor," unpublished manuscript, University of Rochester, October 1979.

8 SUMMARY, CONCLUSIONS, AND FUTURE DIRECTIONS

We suggested at the outset of our analysis that politicians could be usefully analyzed as brokers of wealth changes in the polity. Our analysis was intended as an extension of the interest-group theory of government, which stresses the generation of wealth changes among voters as a primary driving force of political behavior. At this point it is hoped the reader would agree that the middleman analogy leads to a fruitful analysis of politics, but it is perhaps still useful to summarize some of our major results before proceeding to discuss some of the future directions of this type of research.

One obvious result that we can claim is that the tools of microeconomics (supply and demand) can be applied to the legislative process. The application of microeconomics to politics is, of course, not novel, but as far as we are aware, the modeling of the behavior of interest groups in procuring influence from legislators in terms of supply and demand analysis is a relatively new approach. Our analysis of the demand and supply of wealth transfers (and of legislation generally) stresses the theoretical and empirical (across state governments in the United States) importance of certain constitutionally determined

123

aspects of legislative organization in the wealth-transfer process. Most notably, the overall size of the legislature and the ratio of house sizes, along with other economic characteristics of political jurisdictions (e.g., population), predictably impact on the observed levels of wealth transfers and general legislative activities across states.

With this general model of wealth transfers in hand, our analysis turned to the consideration of the factors that go into an explanation of the compensation of politicians as middlemen. There were basically four parts of this analysis.

First, we examined the determinants of the legal pay of politicians. In particular, we examined the monopoly power that is possessed by legislators in cases where they can set their own level of legitimate pay versus cases where it is set in the constitution. As follows predictably from a special application of monopoly theory in this case, we find a high degree of monopoly power in legislator wages in pay-by-statute states. Thus, even though legislators are brokers in the wealth-transfer process, they may gain sizeable rents from performing this function.

Second, legal pay is clearly not the only pay that politicians receive for brokering wealth changes among voters. Yet the extralegal pay of politicians is not directly observable. To get at the problem of the pattern of extralegal pay among politicians, then, we devised and tested a theory of the occupational composition of legislatures that yields some indirect evidence on this problem. In essence, we presented a theory of the labor supply of politicians based on the argument that there will be a predictable ordering of the supply prices of legislators from various occupational backgrounds that is inversely related to their ability to combine legislative service with outside income. At low rates of legal pay lawyers and business professionals tend to dominate elections and legislatures because of their ability to earn outside income as legislators. As legal pay increases, the present value of seats tilts in favor of those in occupations, most prominently farmers and housewives, where they are not as proficient in earning outside income by means of internalizing to themselves the direct returns from passing legislation. This theory is strongly supported in a data set on the occupational composition of state legislatures in the United States, and the results provide us with a basis for making some reasonable inferences about the pattern and extent of extralegal pay across legislative settings. Other things equal, we would expect extralegal activities to be more important in cases where the legal pay for legislators is low.

Third, we analyzed the nature of competition for rents within political parties. We found essentially that larger majorities are associated with more competition for the rents and therefore with lower pay for majority leaders. Competition from "within" is therefore a pronounced force in party politics.

Fourth, we considered the executive branch as the monitor of the wealth-transfer activities of the legislature. The chief executive has bargaining power in the bilateral relationship with the legislature because he has to sign legislation. We postulate simply that this bargaining power is greater where the gains of the legislative wage cartel are greater, and we find strong support for this proposition in an empirical examination of gubernatorial pay in the United States.

These conclusions, then, are some of the major things that we have learned thus far in our studies of political institutions. It is hoped these analyses represent some useful building blocks toward a positive-predictive theory of state action. As in all scientific work, however, answers to one set of questions only serve to raise other questions. In this regard we would like to conclude by considering an important area for future research on the rationale of political institutions.

Throughout our study of wealth transfers and the role that politicians play in brokering wealth transfers, we treated the institutional environment of representative democracy as an exogenous, predetermined set of constraints that confront the economic agents in our theory. The size of the legislature, the term lengths of legislators, the length of the legislative session, the boundaries of legislative districts, the existence of bicameral legislatures, the veto power of the governor, and numerous other aspects of political organization are therefore essentially *unexplained* in our theory. We can explain how these institutions affect variables such as legislator pay and the occupational composition of legislatures, but we have not offered an independent explanation of these institutions. This, of course, is not an unusual deficiency in a microeconomic study. Something has to be taken as given, and this something is typically the institutional constraint set confronting the economic actor. When we analyze, for example, the behavior of consumers in a private-property, private-market setting, we presuppose the existence of a legal-contractual system conducive to market exchange. Our point here is that one way of defining progress in economic theory, and particularly in the economic theory of political organizations, is the degree to which one can pierce this institutional veil and discover the underlying rationale for how the rules of political organization came to be established. In this regard the literature on public choice and the economic approach to politics offers us two approaches.

The first approach, personified in the important works of Buchanan and Rawls, is a normative approach to constitutional choice.[1] This approach is based on the premise that the fairest set of social rules is the one that a rational individual would choose were this individual devoid of information about his possible future position in the society that he is creating. At base this methodology provides for an ethical analysis of constitutional choice and suggests that fairness, defined as unbiased choice, should be an important ingredient in the derivation of a social contract. If such a concept of equity is generally accepted, then it is by all means reasonable to analyze existing institutional arrangements from the perspective of such a concept. However, it is extremely doubtful whether such analysis will make a perceptible difference in the character of prevailing institutions. Normative theory is useful in helping us clarify our norms, but it is another question whether such analysis will impact on the pattern of real institutional development.

The fact that the normative approach to social choice may not be terribly helpful in the task of explaining social and political institutions leads us back to our primary concern in this book, which is to analyze political choice using positive economics as a guide. Ethical theories may have good guys and bad guys, but economic theory possesses no such distinctions. Economic theory is about the children of Adam Smith, who obey the dictates of self-interest, given the constraints on their behavior that prevail. In this approach it is not enough to say that institutions are god-given or that the world is the way it is because it was made that way. Understanding institutional choice in this way requires starting with self-interested individuals and seeing how the invisible hand works in the choice of institutions and rules of the game. In contrast to the normative approach to social choice, this approach would suggest that individuals are not neutral in their choice of institutions. They are self-interested, and we would expect to see the manifestation of this self-interest in the design of social institutions.

There is thus a sharp contrast in the two approaches to constitutional-institutional analysis. It is also fair to say, however, that at this point in time the normative approach to constitutional analysis is much better developed in the literature than the positive approach. Indeed, as adherents of the positive approach, we have no positive analysis of constitutions to present to the reader at this time.[2] For the present we have to confine ourselves to offering a few of the preliminary ideas that we think are important in going about the development of a positive theory of social choice.

First, in applying the positive approach, it is crucial to figure out the impact of existing institutions. Landes and Posner argue that the impact of an independent judiciary is to make special-interest laws more durable.[3] From this observation they are able to argue that the judiciary is equivalent to a long-term contracting device in the interest-group theory of government. Their basic theory is not important to us here, but their approach is. If the impact of institutions can be discovered, we can figure out who wins and who loses from the way institutions are designed. In this way positive explanations of institutional processes can be deduced.

Of course, the problem in this approach is that there are numerous hypotheses that will explain the function of a given institution. In the Landes-Posner theory both "good" and "bad" laws can be made more durable by independent judges. The trick, therefore, in applying positive analysis to institutional choice is to present theories in a testable form so that alternative hypotheses can be ruled out. When dealing with such things as constitutions, this is not as easy as it sounds, but some progress is being made along these lines.[4]

A second general point about analyzing constitutional choice is that we would expect the citizen-consumer-taxpayer to play a larger role in constitutional processes than in normal political processes. The reason for this resides in the net expected benefits facing the individual in the two cases. Constitutions are more durable than any one politician or group of politicians, and the individual voter's stake is thus larger when considering constitutional issues. At the relevant margins of behavior, then, we expect more voter impact on constitutions than on regular elections. It is conceivable, of course, that the impact of voters on constitutions may still be trivial compared to that of well-organized interest groups. After all, we have government because we have constitutions, and we have argued that government amounts to a scheme for wealth redistributions that are generally antithetical to consumer-voter interests.

A third point about the positive analysis of institutions relates to the role of incumbent politicians in these processes. These individuals typically play a major role in constitution writing and revision, and it would not be out of line with the preceding analysis in this volume to suggest that this is not because legislators have a comparative advantage at writing laws. After all, there is a competitive supply of lawyers to draft legislation. There is also no particular reason to feel that politicians are the great repository of wisdom about how to make government function "better." It is thus quite feasible to argue that incumbent politicians who may be able to resist the entry of new political competition can write the rules of the game in a way that is favorable to their expected earnings as brokers of subsequent wealth transfers embodied in normal legislation. Consider, for example, that this approach can rationalize the predominance of single-member constituencies and the absence of extensive competition among incumbent politicians in U.S. political institutions.[5]

A final point to recognize about constitutions is that they are not typically immutable documents. Indeed, virtually all constitutions have amendment procedures built into them. One way to study constitutions is thus to study how they are amended and rewritten over time. Perhaps, as outlined previously, voters have a heavy influence on the design of the original constitution, but incumbent politicians and interest groups control the amendment process and systematically alter the rules in their favor in subsequent periods. Landes-Posner and Crain-Tollison have argued as much in two recent papers.[6] Be this as it may, the point is to stress the importance of analyzing the constitutional revision process, and in this regard, like the other substantive parts of this book, state constitutions in the United States provide a natural cross-sectional laboratory for such analysis.

This represents a small sample of the considerations that we feel are important in developing a positive theory of the constraints that bind us into a society. This is obviously not a route toward a romantic theory of government as a munificent institution. It is a route toward a hard-edged theory of government that can be subjected to rigorous empirical testing.

NOTES

1. See, in particular, James M. Buchanan and Gordon Tullock, *The Calculus of Consent* (Ann Arbor: University of Michigan Press, 1962); and John Rawls, *A Theory of Justice* (Cambridge, Mass.: Harvard University Press, 1971).

2. We are, however, presently in the process of conducting such an examination of state constitutional processes in the United States.

3. William Landes and Richard Posner, "The Independent Judiciary in an Interest-Group Perspective," *Journal of Law and Economics* 18 (December 1975):875–901.

4. See W. Mark Crain and Robert D. Tollison, "Constitutional Change in an Interest-Group Perspective," *Journal of Legal Studies* 8 (January 1979):165–75.

5. See W. Mark Crain, "On the Structure and Stability of Political Markets," *Journal of Political Economy* 85 (August 1977):829–42.

6. Landes and Posner, "The Independent Judiciary in an Interest-Group Perspective;" and Crain and Tollison, "Constitutional Change in an Interest-Group Perspective."

NAME INDEX

SUBJECT INDEX

133